MW01108113

RENEWING

YOUR CHRISTIAN SELF

~WISDOM FROM THE LIVES OF WOMEN

IN THE OLD AND NEW TESTAMENTS~

A Woman's Study

Cheryl Dickow

Cover Artist Lara M. Sabatini

God blesses each and every one of us with friends, family, and acquaintances who often challenge us to grow as Christians and make our journey an anointed, rewarding one. He gives us people in our lives for a reason, a season, or a lifetime.

To ask Cheryl to speak at your event,
or to find the finest in
Christian fiction and non-fiction,
please visit our website

www.BezalelBooks.com

Other books by Cheryl Dickow include:

Elizabeth: A Holy Land Pilgrimage

Raising Christian Children in a Secular World: Christian Parenting (revised April, 2007)

Printed in the United States of America

ISBN 978-0-9794976-1-2

Dearest Sister in Christ,

I write this book with the full and complete belief that, as women, our lives are more beautiful, more bountiful, than the world would like us to believe. I encourage you to take the time, to learn Scripture, and to come to that same understanding. In that knowledge you will be most fully alive. My prayer for you is that the realization of God's truth in your life be full and complete so that your existence, while pleasing to Him, is also pleasing to yourself. My suggestion is to read this book a section a week. I recommend that you read a new section on Saturday or Sunday and then thoughtfully bring the essence of that section, and its related Scripture, into your life during the following week.

Consider copying the Scripture onto a pretty piece of stationary, onto brightly colored index cards, or into a small journal that you are able to keep with you throughout the week. As you copy the words, remind yourself that they are the words of God. Praise Him and thank Him for them. If they inspire you to look up and add new Scripture verses, by all means do so! Then, as the week progresses, continually read the words to yourself so that they become committed in your mind and heart. Although you might not literally memorize them, allow them to easily and comfortably settle into your spirit. They will connect you to the Lord in a beautiful way.

This book is written so that each week continues to build, adding new knowledge, thoughts, and Scripture to your life. According to the bible, the Father's desire is to have an intimate, loving relationship with each of us. When we study the Old and New Testaments we are able to develop that relationship because we acquire knowledge and understand the Lord in more meaningful ways. We begin to measure our lives differently and truly understand that helping each other is helping ourselves. We see the truth in Jesus' words that we will reap what we sow.

When you are finished reading all the sections, you will have embraced some of the beautiful messages that our sisters in faith have brought us through His Word. You will have a renewed sense of joy and energy for whatever God is offering you. May this book make you hunger and thirst for the Word of God in a new and deeper way.

Cheryl Dickow

Table of Contents

"The hour is coming, in fact has come, when the vocation of women is being acknowledged in its fullness, the hour in which women acquire in the world an influence, an effect and a power never hitherto achieved. This is why, at this moment when the human race is undergoing so deep a transformation, women imbued with a spirit of the Gospel can do so much to aid humanity in not falling."

John Paul II in his Apostolic Letter on the Dignity and Vocation of Women, Mulieris Dignitatem

In the "unity of the two," man and woman are called from the beginning not only to exist "side by side" or "together," but they are also called to exist mutually "one for the other."

Mulieris Dignitatem

A Woman's Worth

From Eve to Sarah to Deborah to Mary, Scripture assures every woman who has ever lived that her life is both special and valuable. Her life has a purpose and a meaning set by God and necessary to His plan for humankind. Each and every one of us came here with an extraordinary set of gifts and a particular set of circumstances. Our births were the intentional acts of an affectionate, devoted God whose love for us is truly immeasurable. We are as unique and varied as the stars in the sky. Our gifts and talents are limitless.

The seasons of our lives are a thing of beauty and honor. We may lead or we may follow. Some of us will feel exhilarated while others of us will feel exhausted. And then the experiences reverse. And those whose time it is to reap will reap while those whose time it is to sow will sow. We share more than a common faith heritage with the women of the bible. Yesterday, today, and tomorrow we remain the same in that our life has an anointed meaning and a distinct purpose.

We may lose sight of this reality in all our "busy-ness" but it, our precious life, never loses a meaning and purpose set by God. God shares the stories of the women in our faith history to let us know that, while our sojourns are very much our own, they are not new. And, in this, we all become equal in His eyes. Like a parent who marvels at her ability to love each of her children so fully, so completely, so it is with God's love for us. Each and every one of us enjoys His full and complete love. He is enamored with us, one and all. As we embark on our pilgrimage, searching for Truth, Scripture calls us to look deep into the lives of the women whose stories are told. Scripture beckons us, knowing that we can be touched by His precious words, His beloved heroines.

In Scripture we see courageous women, warrior women, and women rulers. Some women in Scripture have been embraced while others have been cast out. Women have brought both evil and salvation. Women, the Word of God shows us, are the embodiment of strength and ability in some of the most vulnerable of situations. They can save or destroy nations. Their fortitude is awe-inspiring. While teaching us about their own lives we find that they teach us about our lives as well.

Women of Scripture speak to us in familiar and loving ways. They know our struggles and reach to us in their stories. They help us learn how to live a life pleasing to God and yet fulfilling for ourselves. We find assurance that our own uniqueness is both expected and nurtured. In studying and understanding Scripture we come to see that these women, these role models, all have their own special relationship with God. Some women have had the audacity to be in disobedience to God while others are in complete obedience. Some argue and chortle at God while others revere His existence. In the end, each and every woman's relationship with God is wonderfully her own. In this way, no woman is left without a heroine. Whether she is homemaker or warrior, her predecessor is in Scripture. We see silent women, joyful women, powerful women, repentant women, and wily women.

Through it all we continue to be assured that each and every woman whose mention appears in a verse, a paragraph, a chapter, or a book is there for a reason. Her story might be our story. Her story might be our best friend's story or our sister's story. Her story exists for a reason just as she existed for a reason: just as each of us exists for a reason. For His reason we came into being and for His reason we move forward into the world. We, too, are courageous women and warrior women and women rulers.

We, too, are silent women, joyful women, repentant women, and wily women. We understand that God put before us life and death, and we chose life. Every day we rise to the challenge and draw strength from the knowledge that only with God will our roles be truly fulfilled and fulfilling. If we fail to do our job, or reach our destiny, we leave a hole in God's plan. No one, we will see, can do what each of us is uniquely called to do. We are different for a reason: His reason. Embracing the Word of God allows us to embrace our own individuality. So, whether it is in our home, in our relationships, at work, or in some distant corner of the world, our purpose is ours alone. An opportunity to be most fully alive is found in achieving that purpose.

In sharing with us His anointed examples of the women in our faith history, God shares with us His understanding of our struggles and His support of us in our journey. He reminds us how uniquely He made us. He comforts us through our pain and cheers us through our successes. And while He does not promise us a life without distress, He does give us His word that He will be with us during distressing times. When we learn the ways of our creator we find that nothing else is able to empower us like that knowledge. We are special to God and He uses the Old and New Testament alike to embrace us and to nurture us as no earthly being could. He is our God, our Creator, and our Redeemer. He speaks to us in Scripture. His Word is our answer, regardless of the question. And it all began with our creation.

"Then God said: "Let us make man in our image, after our likeness. Let them have dominion over the fish of the sea, the birds of the air, and the cattle, and over all the wild animals and all the creatures that crawl on the ground." God created man in his image; in the divine image he created him; male and female he created them.

In this beautiful telling of the creation of man and woman we hear God speaking, we hear Him formulating plans for our existence. Right away we notice that God refers to Himself as "us" and "our." The entire creation process involved the Father, the Son, and the Holy Spirit as we clearly see in Genesis 1:26. By using the pronouns "us" and "our," God immediately makes clear His connection to the Son and to the Spirit. Just as it would be unwise to separate, or to prioritize, the Father, the Son, and the Holy Spirit, it would also be unwise to prioritize the value of God's creation of man and woman.

Indeed, we could no more separate a woman's role from a man's role in humanity than we could separate the Father from the Son or the Spirit. Unlike the secular world that has often misinterpreted the creation verses, God's purposeful use of the pronouns "us," "our," and "them" gives women their inherent worth. Women do not need laws and amendments to gain respect or authority. God gives us all we need in the story of creation when He says, "Let **them** have dominion...(my emphasis)." He shows that our creation is as integral to His plan as is His existence to the Son and to the Spirit.

When we are in union with Christ-like men or in friendships with Christ-like women or working with Christ-minded co-workers we find our worth unquestioned. As Christians we are also called to be those exact same things to others: Christ-like spouses, Christ-like peers and co-workers, and Christ-like friends. We are all valued and respected as co-creations of God and have an obligation to bring that realization to one another. To receive this truth we must also give this truth to others. Our life, then, is filled with reason and purpose. Our journey is blessed and anointed as we take on the task of bringing God's love and light to others through our compassion, joy, kindness, patience, and perseverance.

However, living in a secular world has taken us off our intended path. And in so doing has minimized our inherent worth in Christ who so believed in our intrinsic value that He willingly died for us. We sometimes find our life's purpose in direct opposition to our worldly existence. We are often receiving mixed opinions and are reluctantly following advice that changes from day to day. It is no wonder that people are flocking, in droves, to anyone who has a viable message of love and happiness. God created us to be both receivers and deliverers of His love. It is part of our nature to seek out love because our original source of that love is God Himself.

But in our pursuit of that fulfillment we ought to be wary of words that are not in compliance with Scripture and His ways. This is why time spent studying the Word is invaluable. We come to know Him through the bible and are able to discern the messages of today. Many women today are turning, or returning, to their Creator for His vision of their lives. We are inspiring one another and understand the role we played during Jesus' time on earth and throughout church history.

Indeed, women today are yearning to carry on the tradition handed to them by their sisters-in-faith. We are finding a renewed sense of self as we embrace the wisdom found in the Scripture. In turning back to God's Word, as our source of insight and guidance, we find the support we crave. In Scripture we find heroines of every shape, size, and color. We find ourselves encouraged as only God can, with love, kindness, and understanding. We find the reason for our being. From Scripture, we can rest assured that our worth, in God's eyes, is no less (and no more) than man's.

Our society has gone myriad ways in regards to women's roles and women's rights but not so with Scripture. It was said quickly, and early on, that a woman's worth was sacred. A woman is held in the highest esteem in God's eyes. Her work is both necessary and sacred to God's plan for the world. It is a message that we should humbly acknowledge. Genesis 2:20b-23 adds another dimension to the creation of woman that is just as profound as Genesis 1:26-27.

> *But for Adam no suitable helper was found. So the Lord God caused the man to fall into a deep sleep; and while he was sleeping, he took one of the man's ribs and closed up the place with flesh. Then the Lord God made a woman from the rib he had taken out of the man, and he brought her to the man. The man said, "This is now bone of my bones and flesh of my flesh, she shall be called 'woman,' for she was taken out of man."*

Without woman, man was incomplete. God's plans for humanity could not yet be accomplished. Just as the Father is only complete with the Son and with the Spirit, man is only complete with woman.

There was much to fill man's world and yet the need for the creation of woman was evident. It was woman, and nothing else, that would complete man's existence or more pointedly, complete God's plan. They were to work together to build God's kingdom on earth. Ultimately these sagacious creation verses impress upon us our intrinsic worth. They ring peacefully in our ears and rest softly in our hearts. They are the food of our infant daughters and the nourishment of our sisters and friends. When we raise our daughters in this understanding and remind our friends of their inherent worth in Christ, we give them an awareness that can forever impact their existence.

When we encourage one another to recognize and satisfy our longing for God with God Himself, we allow each other to be free from misplaced priorities. Being free from misplaced priorities allows us to embrace our lives with revived hope and joy. Jesus left us with peace and it is in that peace we are able to live most abundantly. There is great and lasting comfort in knowing how vital we are to God's plan for the world. We need to be free from worldly messages that take us off our path to God. We will see from the women of Scripture that God's plan cannot unfold without each and every one of us. Our life was a purposeful gift from God. What we do with our lives is a gift we give back to Him.

Each woman in scripture has a beautifully unique story that should open our eyes and our hearts to the variety of roles that we will play in our lives. If we have allowed ourselves to be truly blessed, our earthly friendships will also reflect this diversity. We will have friends who are feisty and friends that are complacent. We will know women who are outspoken and courageous as well as women who are withdrawn and content (which is often a courageous statement in and of itself!). They are all a part of our lives, as we are of theirs, to bring completion and wholeness. We should inspire one another, console one another, and support one another regardless of our individual journeys.

Sadly, we often find ourselves at great odds with each other. We have been polarized in ways that are an affront to the God who calls upon us to love one another. We are jealous and envious when we should be supportive and enthusiastic. Working mothers find themselves in opposition to stay-at-home mothers. Mothers who choose public schools have been pitted against mothers who choose to home-school. Women who support themselves are pitted against women who are supported by their husbands. Women who marry have been put at odds with women who stay single. The list seems to grow with each passing year.

Indeed, the secular world has done a wonderful job in dividing women, one against the other, and in so doing has made a mockery of the plan God had in mind for each one of us. It seems as if we have forgotten the simplest of all commandments: The Golden Rule. In the end it appears as if we have forsaken both ourselves as well as those people that God has placed in our lives. From this dire position, the secular world offers us a new-age remedy, often wrapped in the cloak of Christianity. We are encouraged to follow self-help books with ever-changing advice.

Instead, in our quest for Truth, let us be running to the Word of God as our reliable source of guidance and wisdom. Let us measure all we hear, all we read, and all we see against the Truth of Scripture; for it alone provides the fullness that we seek. Jesus, we know, is the Truth that sets us free. We should be drawn to those people who direct us to our Creator, our source of life, and His word. All else falls short. More than ever before the often used phrase that heeds us to look out for a wolf in sheep's clothing seems appropriate.

We should, as Christian women, purposely replace the secularly accepted words like "universal being" and "ultimate power" with the correct reference to God. We, then, start to become the witnesses that Jesus expects us to be. When we remind ourselves that, upon His resurrection, Jesus first appeared to a woman, we are also reminded of His call on our life to be His witnesses. We then become instruments that God is able to use in a meaningful way. When we strengthen our love of one another and ourselves (in a non-narcissistic way) we are more fully participating in God's unique plan for our life and the abundant grace that He gives us to bring His plan to fruition.

When we draw our understanding and wisdom from scripture we will find that there is a plan for the likes of each and every one of us, in every phase of our life. We will all find the heroines that God has provided in His word. We will recognize that different seasons of our life require these different heroines, each with their own unique characteristics and personality.

In that way, Scripture becomes our lifeblood. Scripture connects each of us to God through all the times in our life. In God's Word we will see our friends and we will see our neighbors. We will see that we are created as loving beings that should bolster one another. We will cherish the great diversity that exists in the paths of our lives. Scripture will show us what is truly important and help us set our ways in accordance with God's mandates. Scripture will kindly show us our struggles are not new. Through God's Word we will find women that are just like us: women on a journey.

Lord,

May I always be guided by the examples
You have given me in Scripture.

May I understand my immense worth in Your eyes
and my value to my family, friends, and neighbors.

May my life unfold as You have chosen,
which I know to be a life
pleasing to You, of service to others,
and full of joy and peace.

I ask this all in Him,
with Him,
And
through Him.

Amen

The Word of God

Above all, love each other deeply, because love covers over a multitude of sins. Offer hospitality to one another without grumbling. Each one should use whatever gift he has received to serve others, faithfully administering God's grace in its various forms. 1 Peter 4:8-10

And we know that in all things God works for the good of those who love him, who have been called according to his purpose. Romans 8:28

For anyone who does not love his brother, whom he has seen, cannot love God, whom he has not seen. And he has given us this command: Whoever loves God must also love his brother. 1 John 4:20-21

Nobody should seek his own good, but the good of others. 1 Corinthians 10:24

For this God is our God for ever and ever; he will be our guide even to the end. Psalm 48:14

Commit to the Lord whatever you do, and your plans will succeed. Proverbs 16:3

The Lord bless you and keep you! The Lord let his face shine upon you, and be gracious to you! The Lord look upon you kindly and give you peace! Numbers 6:24-26

Affirming Your Worth

Meditate on the Scripture passages in this section and then write your own affirmation sentence. Your affirmation should reflect your innate worth in Christ. Throughout this coming week, begin and end every day with your affirmation sentence. Say it quietly to yourself throughout the day. Make your affirmation sentence reverberate in every cell in your body.

In Christ I ...

_____

_____

_____

_____

_____

_____

_____

_____

_____

_____

Being a person in the image and likeness of God thus also involves existing in a relationship, in relation to the other "I." This is a prelude to the definitive self-revelation of the Triune God: a living unity in the communion of the Father, Son and Holy Spirit.

Mulieris Dignitatem

The Holy Spirit

Before we can even begin to look at all the interesting and wonderful women of Scripture, we must first look at our relationship with the Holy Spirit. The Holy Spirit connects the created to the Creator in the most intimate of ways. Women, when moved by the Spirit, are powerful forces. They become fully equipped to do the work of God with both His blessing and His anointing.

Unfortunately, we have been programmed to tune out all the messages and intuitions and hunches that would otherwise fill our being. Intuitions and messages and hunches that would allow our lives to be filled with graces and abound in blessings. We have tuned out, turned off, and generally abandoned a beautiful way that the Lord has always chosen to work with us. A gift that has always been ours has been sullied and ridiculed by so many people that we have found it easier to walk away.

Many of us have allowed the secular world to dominate our existence and in so doing have filled our lives with what appears to be more but is actually less: less hope, less faith, less fulfillment, and less integrity. In following today's example of "busy-ness" many of us have abandoned our spiritual selves for our secular selves.

Indeed, our everyday lives are filled with more things to do and less time in which to do them. We are encouraged to eat on the run, feed our children on the run, and in general be "on-the-run." And with this new way of life, this new "busy-ness," we are less inclined to follow the Spirit when the Spirit moves us. We are less likely to hear the Spirit when He calls. We brush aside those inclinations in our mad dash to accomplish 25 hours worth of work in a 24-hour day. Inclinations that would allow us to carry out the work of God as we move through the world no longer guide us. We have lost the time to stop and listen to the still, small voice of God speaking to our spirit.

According to Romans 8, in living by our nature we set our minds upon our natural desires. However, when we live by the Spirit, we set our minds on what the Spirit desires. So, in coasting along with secular values and ways, our natural desires begin to replace and dominate our spiritual desires. In essence we unknowingly, or unwittingly, lose track of our spiritual selves.

When we are caught up in the "busy-ness" of our lives we are unable, or less likely, to produce the fruits of the Spirit: the fruits by which Christ will know us. Galatians 5:22 identifies these fruits as love, joy, peace, patience, kindness, goodness, faithfulness, gentleness and self-control. The very characteristics that are neither embraced nor encouraged by our secular world are the only characteristics that set us apart as followers of Jesus.

In Scripture we are told to *carry each other's burdens, and in this way you will fulfill the law of Christ. (Galatians 6:2).* The mandates in Scripture quite clearly tell us how to conduct our lives. While our society often encourages us to care for ourselves and to "win at all costs," Scripture directs us to care for each other and in that way recognize that we are fulfilling the laws of Christ. When Christ said that there would always be the poor and disadvantaged among us, He was sharing His understanding of our difficulty in serving others. Most certainly this is not what He wants, but He knows that for almost all of us, this is a real struggle; to subjugate our own selves for the sake of others. And when He died for us He gave us the consummate example of serving our fellow man.

Fortunately, when we make a point to develop our spiritual selves, the Spirit will be able to guide us in priceless ways. Let me share a story about myself and Pam...

One hot, late July afternoon I decided to take a walk around my neighborhood. The sweltering weather was made even more so by the fact that I was overdue with my second child. As I wobbled around the block, pulling my two-year-old son in a wagon, I noticed a young mother planting flowers near the front of her home. She didn't look up as I passed but continued planting her flowers.

I circled the block once and, as I neared my own drive, felt inclined to circle the block again. There was no real reason to do this as neither my son, nor I, was enjoying this stroll. Nonetheless I avoided walking up my driveway and continued on with a few steps that would change my life forever.

As I rounded the block a second time all my senses were focused on the heat, my overdue pregnancy, and my complaining son. Out of the blue I heard a sweet voice say, "You look like you could use some lemonade." Although normally quite reserved this invitation seemed to hit a chord with me and I uncharacteristically accepted the kind offer. The thought of resting my feet and letting my son out of the wagon was just what I needed.

As it turned out, the invitation came from that young mother who had been diligently planting her flowers. We sat, laughed at the dilemmas of young children, talked of the weather, and went our separate ways.

Two days later I gave birth to my second son and, to my delight and surprise, received a beautiful bowl of fruit from the lady with whom I had shared a much-needed refreshing glass of lemonade. With the fruit she also gave me a beautiful book about raising sons (she has three of them) which I have enjoyed over and over again.

Make no mistake about it, the Spirit will move our life's circumstances, and us, in priceless ways...

It was late July and Pam's flowers were long overdue for planting. She finally found the time to work on them and was bound and determined to get the job done. The plants needed to get into the ground if they were going to survive. If not, she would have to throw them all out.

As she got to work she noticed a VERY pregnant lady walking in the street. The lady was pulling a little boy in a red wagon. It was quite hot and neither of them looked like they were enjoying the walk. As they passed her driveway the Holy Spirit urged her to speak to the pregnant lady, to say "hello." She resisted the urge as the flower matter was quite pressing. She really wanted to get this job done and enjoy the garden. She didn't want to lose the flowers. And so she let the lady pass by.

Pam continued working industriously when she noticed the lady passing by a second time. The little boy seemed more miserable than before and the lady looked like she was going to deliver at any moment. This time the Holy Spirit was quite insistent. "Speak to her!" And so she put her trowel down, looked up and said, "You look like you could use some lemonade."

And from those inclinations, both hers to offer lemonade and mine to take a second walk around the block, God has forged a most beautiful friendship: a friendship that has lasted fifteen years and several moves. A friendship that now sees children graduating from college, getting married, and having children of their own. A truly blessed friendship orchestrated by the Holy Spirit.

I share this story to illustrate that when we allow it, the Holy Spirit will orchestrate much in our lives. From our relationships to our careers to our finances, there is nothing in our lives that we need to keep from the Holy Spirit. But having gotten out of touch with our natural ability to listen to the spirit and nurture our relationship to God, we spend time spinning our wheels. We invest our energy in things that were never meant to be and on roads that we were never meant to travel. We look to a world with a one-size-fits-all belief when we are, in fact, so customized that one size could never even fit two, let alone all.

Getting caught up in our secular existence also hinders our ability to produce the fruits of the spirit. These fruits are considered love, joy, peace, patience, kindness, generosity, faithfulness, gentleness, and self-control. We will see, as we study the women of the Bible, that these fruits always seem to make their presence known. And, maybe more importantly, we recognize that God continues to provide ways for each woman, along with ourselves, to manifest these fruits based upon the circumstances of life. We also see how life is filled with opportunities to make us believe that these fruits are not necessary, or to invalidate their worth. We might find ourselves, like many of the women in Scripture, more apt to feel pangs of jealousy or pride than peace and kindness. It is in these times that we are most able to call upon Christ and redeem these moments for Him and for His cross. We then, as He has said, will find our rewards to be of the heavenly kind. When, in our darkest hour, we are able to be most like Christ, we will see that the fruits we bear are truly from the Spirit. We do not manifest them; the Spirit manifests them so that through us His kingdom is known.

When a woman frets over her identity in the secular world, she is less apt to produce the fruits that would have been more readily available to her on her own walk in life. When she finds herself in heated competition with others, she is often unable to be an instrument for God.

We all like the idea of being valuable and full of merit and regrettably buy into the erroneous notion that we are not as valuable as our "successful" counterparts, whoever they may be. We mistakenly measure success by secular standards and consider ourselves on the short end of the stick. We often forget that we were created **with** man and mistakenly think we should be **like** man. As we try to become more like "man" we begin to lose our instincts and capabilities as "woman." In forgetting who we were created to be we lose out on our real purpose for living. In vying for what the world tells us are "limited spots" for success, we forget that the God we serve has no limits.

Another very significant part of our distinctive sojourn is to seek and understand our own unique gifts as well as the gifts from the Holy Spirit. These gifts are different from the fruits of the Spirit but are just as necessary in our walk as Christians. Furthermore, it becomes crucial for us to understand St. Paul's message regarding all these gifts. When accepted, these gifts become the sustenance of our spiritual existence and invaluable tools to ensure the success of our life's journey and walk with Christ. And, as St. Paul writes in 1 Corinthians 12, these gifts, unless motivated by love, become useless and invalid. They were given from the Father, with great love, and are ours to share with others with the same great love. Love, of course, being a fruit of the Spirit!

The gifts from the Holy Spirit include wisdom, understanding, counsel, knowledge, fortitude, piety, and fear of the Lord. These gifts, while valuable for our earthly existence, are meant to glorify His kingdom and for the propagation of our faith and the Good News. Additionally, these gifts allow us to achieve the relationship with God that He so very much desires.

Wisdom helps us know and seek God. Wisdom separates our thoughts and our actions from the foolish and the arrogant. Wisdom guides us on our journey as we understand our true ineptness without God. In wisdom King Solomon ruled God's people, without wisdom he succumbed to the temptations of the world. Wisdom is not a once-in-a-lifetime acquisition but a life long expedition that has many bumps along the way.

Understanding allows us to use both our heart and our head. Understanding works with wisdom as we make choices and decisions that are in keeping with God's edicts. We understand the value of a life that is pleasing to God and are wise enough to make that overall choice but also wise in the day-to-day choices that make up our lives. We understand the need to use both our compassion and our intellect when we make our decisions and as such are more apt to please God.

When we seek good *counsel* we show maturity and a level headedness that is in keeping with God's ways. When we provide good *counsel* we are sharing our wisdom and understanding of God with others to help them make decisions that are based upon the Lord's edicts and ways. We are bringing glory to His kingdom on earth.

Knowledge is gaining information about God and using it as He would like. When we are knowledgeable we are more inclined to be in a right relationship with God and with others. When we are steeped in the Word, we are able to draw upon that knowledge in our daily lives.

Fortitude is that trait that allows our faith and our hope to move us through the times of our lives, having the knowledge that God works all things for His good. *Fortitude* helps us run the race set before us so that we make it to the finish line!

Piety is a beautiful reverence for our Creator. Piety allows us to be humble as we recognize His hand always in our lives. A pious attitude is never one of arrogance or judgment. Instead, a pious attitude is one of great humility as it shows our understanding and awareness of the awesome God we serve.

Fear of the Lord is that realization of our deep need to have God in our lives and the fear of ever separating ourselves from Him. In coming full circle, Proverbs 1:7 identifies that fear of the Lord is the beginning of wisdom!

These gifts from the Holy Spirit (wisdom, understanding, counsel, knowledge, fortitude, piety, and fear of the Lord) are ours as followers of Christ. The same Spirit that led Christ into the wilderness is ours to lead us from this wilderness to Christ. We need to be led by the Spirit in this life if this life is to be in accordance with God's plans.

Throughout Scripture we see women working in accordance with the Spirit, bearing fruits of the Spirit, and displaying the gifts of the Spirit. We see plans unfolding and lives guided in a rich and fulfilling way. Scripture reiterates the point that each of us will have our own particular blessings: blessings as unique as we are. But while our blessings are unique and our talents are ours alone, we are all gifted in the Spirit. It is that Spirit, His Spirit, which tries to move us in ways that are both pleasing to the Lord and satisfying to our journey.

Holy Spirit,

You are the third person in the blessed Trinity.

Your love for me is as great as
the Father's and the Son's.

Your interest in my life
is as great as the Father's and the Son's.

Let my life be pleasing
to the Father and to the Son
through your guidance.

Let our relationship be as strong as
my relationship to the Father and to the Son.

Let my thoughts, words, and actions
reflect Your loving presence in my life.

Amen

The Word of God

Now if we are children, then we are heirs-heirs of God and co-heirs with Christ, if indeed we share in his sufferings in order that we may also share in his glory. Romans 8:17

But God chose the foolish things of the world to shame the wise; God chose the weak things of the world to shame the strong. 1 Corinthians 1:27

Humility and the fear of the Lord bring wealth and honor and life. Proverbs 22:4

Get Wisdom, get understanding; do not forget my words or swerve from them. Do not forsake wisdom, and she will protect you; love her, and she will watch over you. Wisdom is supreme; therefore get wisdom. Though it cost all you have, get understanding. Proverbs 4:5-7

May the God of hope fill you with all joy and peace as you trust in him, so that you may overflow with hope by the power of the Holy Spirit. Romans 15:13

The Spirit of the Lord will rest on him-the Spirit of wisdom and of understanding, the Spirit of counsel and of power, the Spirit of knowledge and of the fear of the Lord-and he will delight in the fear of the Lord. Isaiah 11:2-3

Now to each one the manifestation of the Spirit is given for the common good. 1 Corinthians 12:7

You are my friends if you do what I command you. I no longer call you slaves, because a slave does not know what his master is doing. I have called you friends, because I have told you everything I have heard from my Father. John 15:14-15

Ask the Holy Spirit to reveal a Scripture verse to you and write that verse here:

_____
_____
_____
_____
_____
_____

Consider why this verse "speaks" to you and record your personal revelation.

_____
_____
_____
_____
_____
_____
_____
_____
_____
_____

Embracing the Holy Spirit

The Holy Spirit is working in your life. Find ways in which you see the Holy Spirit in action. Record at least two experiences this week in which the Holy Spirit moved you to see another person as Christ does: with love.

Make a commitment to let the Holy Spirit become an active part of your life. Spend time meditating upon Scripture passages regarding the fruits of the Spirit (Galatians 5:22) and the gifts of the Spirit (1 Corinthians 12). Record your experiences and revelations.

_____

_____

_____

_____

_____

_____

_____

_____

_____

_____

_____

_____

In the light of Revelation, creation likewise means the beginning of salvation history.

Mulieris Dignitatem

Eve

Eve was the first woman. Her very existence began as a loving effort on God's part. She completed man and was given dominion, with man, in the Garden of Eden. She walked in the Garden of Eden secure in her knowledge of God's love. Like Eve, we too exist because of God's great love for us.

Scripture tells us that God knew us before we were born. It is a telling statement of God's great love for us to imagine that He knew all about our iniquities, shortcomings, and sinful natures and yet loved us into being. If we are parents, it is very much the way we feel about our own children. Our children are able to bring us great joy and great sorrow. Given that knowledge, we would still make the same choices that brought them into our lives.

And so it is with God except He knew us BEFORE we were born. His knowledge was far deeper than ours was with our children. Women expecting their first babies often fantasize about the complete joy that their children will bring. They mark off the days on the calendar with an unparalleled eagerness. They are not counting on the arguments that lay ahead or the difficulty that will come with raising children. Their minds and hearts can only see the good.

But our benevolent Father saw so much more than that before our own births. He knew of the delight He would have in our existence but more so knew of the snarls that were ahead.

God was well aware that we would, like Eve, come into this world with a free will that would allow us to make our own conscious choices. He knew that we would, similar to Eve, make a wide variety of decisions, some good and some bad. Nonetheless, God still willed our existence. He still welcomed our life, knowing that it would be filled with moments both pleasing to Him and moments disappointing to Him. With great anticipation, He still loved us into being.

When we question His love for us we only need to remind ourselves that He knew what our life would hold and still desired our birth. When we wonder if we could ever be worthy of His immense love, we only need to recall His forgiving nature to those who, like us, disappointed Him or put roadblocks in His path. Do we not, if we are parents, feel the same for our children?

Certainly we know of the deep disappointment that our children, or our loved ones, might bring into our life and yet wouldn't we, given the opportunity, still gladly receive them again and again? And so it is with God. He continually embraces our efforts to return to His fold. His love is greater than our most toxic transgressions. He has given us His Son so that we may forever, in claiming our salvation in Christ, be saved. Christ's death allows God's arms to be forever open to us.

Eve's story shows us that when we put our own self-interests before God's we do more harm than good. Our Father in heaven wants the best for us and has provided for all our needs. As He did for Eve, He does for us. She roamed the Garden of Eden with all her needs met. And yet, that didn't seem to be enough. Eve, in the Garden of Eden, could still be tempted. As baptized followers of Christ we will also find that temptation and sin are a very real part of life.

In the dialogue between Jesus and Satan (Matthew 4) we witness the ways in which Satan will try to draw us in and become accomplices in our own downfall. Satan says to Jesus, *"If you are the Son of God tell these stones to become bread."* Of course Jesus is wiser and stronger than Satan's enticement and is able to respond, *"One does not live by bread alone, but by every word that comes forth from the mouth of God."* Satan continues to try to tantalize Jesus but Jesus will not be worn down. In this exchange we become aware of the fact that temptation is a lifelong struggle. The world says to us, *"If you are successful you will drive 'this particular car,'"* or, *"If you are a 'somebody' you will live in 'this kind of house,'* or *"If you are a good parent your kids will have 'this particular amenity.'"* And, like Jesus, we need to be strong against these tantalizing messages: messages that confuse our priorities and take our eyes off God.

We aren't tempted only once in life. We aren't free from future temptation simply because we are able to overcome a particular allure or addiction. Temptation is a part of life and a weakness that Satan will prey upon. The Gospel of Matthew makes that clear.

Eve's experience in the Garden of Eden show us that temptation and sin are very real things. Most certainly, we can understand the appeal of that "one thing" that is beyond our grasp. In all honesty, it would be difficult for us to say that we would have, most assuredly, made better choices than

Eve. Consider our circumstances now. Do we always avoid sin and temptation? We most assuredly do not. So, in that one moment, Eve captured our temptation with hers. She reminded us how vulnerable we can be, even in the most rewarding of circumstances. And so she sinned.

But as we know, God will always work things to His good and so He sent Jesus to conquer sin, but not our sinful nature. That is our cross to bear. And while the secular world would like us to renounce the reality of sin, our Savior requires us to acknowledge it and consequently His redemption. The socially acceptable message leads us to believe that we can redeem ourselves. We are often led to believe that we are that powerful. However, Scripture assures us that redemption comes only when we approach Christ with true repentance.

In Eve's reach for the apple she made a choice that forever changed human history. In believing the ultimate liar, she stepped out of grace and in so doing, brought about the first sin. The consequences of her actions were immense and seemed to throw the human condition into untold turmoil: child bearing was to become painful and the earth was to become unresponsive in its yield. There would forever be enmity between the serpent and Eve's children. Life would be, as we have experienced, filled with strife. Make no mistake, God was clearly letting us know that there would be dire consequences for our sinful actions and that responsibility would always rest upon our own shoulders. Denying our culpability transcends into our own denial of the salvation that Jesus brought. Although unpleasant, and certainly contrary to popular belief, we are sinners.

We live in a world where we are encouraged to attain more, yearn for more, and set materialistic goals. This is why Jesus reminds us that we cannot worship two masters (Matthew 6:24). Indeed, we oftentimes find ourselves being very shortsighted and believe that an earthly treasure has worth. We might buy into the message that possessions will allow us to possess joy. But nothing could be further from the truth. Joy is ours for the taking when we align our lives with God's commands and dictates.

That spot in our heart that God created for His dwelling can only be filled by God Himself. We learn from Eve that, regardless of the temptation, we should never put our interests above God's Word. When we become the kind of self-centered people that are often nurtured and encouraged in our secular world our view becomes myopic. And as we lose sight of the whole picture, we most assuredly lose sight of God. Or, we begin to see God through the societal messages that deny the existence of sin and its consequences. We begin living with a shortsightedness that becomes a detriment to all that God had in mind for our lives. Our sins, we are told, are minor. Or they are insignificant. Or, more appalling, they aren't sins at all. And so we go our merry way, having forgotten that Eve is our first example of sin and its grievous consequences, especially transgressions without repentance.

We sadly forget that God sees, knows, and orchestrates the "bigger" picture while we only experience a fragment. We begin to believe in our own omnipotence and our own omniscience. We make decisions out of alignment with God's edicts and assume that the little fragment of life that we see is life in its entirety. This is the danger of the corporeal message.

It is that fragment of understanding, both in sight and in knowledge, which is too often being fed by our secular world. That segment then, becomes our guide and our focus as we take our eyes off of God and put them on the things that we begin to believe have value. Eve did just that. She took her eyes off of God and focused them on the one thing she couldn't have: something she mistakenly believed had value. And with her focus off God she was easily able to disobey Him. We, then, immediately learn from Eve how very critical it is for us to keep our focus, our undivided attention, on God and His will in our life. We see the consequences of actions that harm our relationship with Him. We see them loud and clear.

Fortunately, we also learn from Eve God's great love for us, sinners. As sinners we are able to accept the redemption that Jesus offers. If we reject the notion of our sinful nature then we ultimately reject the notion of our salvation. We cannot have one without the other. We know the end of the story. We know that God sent His Son so that we could regain our standing with Him. In Eve's story we see that we must always keep our faith in God whose love is bigger, more extensive, than our worst sins while still recognizing our sinful natures. If we accept the biased message in which our God requires little liability from us, we reject Jesus.

We must consider ourselves accountable for our sins while remembering that we serve a God who only wants the best for us. We should remain attentive to our Lord who sees the whole story when we can only see a page. In the end, God knows our struggles and assures us that He will always draw us back to Him, through the Son. God will lead us back to Him when our focus becomes blurry and our reasoning becomes faulty. When we present Him with a repentant heart He welcomes and absolves us. He is a God of love and a God of forgiveness.

Even though our destiny was altered that day in the garden, we know that Eve, like ourselves, was part of God's loving plan. She taught us how to be mindful of our free will. Eve brought God into our lives in a richer way. Because of Eve, our free will is a true testament of our acceptance of God's will and hand in our lives. Through Eve's disobedience we are given use of our own free will in such a way that our choosing God is more pleasing and more meaningful.

The more we move through the world and encounter women from all walks of life, the more we realize that women are strong and resilient creatures. Yes, we make mistakes. But as Christian women we have the full knowledge of God's sanctifying grace in our lives. That knowledge allows us, when our hearts are burdened with sin, to repent and return to His strong arms, wiser and more able to do His will. It is through free will that both our love and repentance are so meaningful.

It is not surprising that women find themselves in situations where their true strength is so often showcased. Women, by their own nature, bring both delicacy and force into the world. They are capable and worthy mothers, neighbors, leaders, and friends. Women are powerful, passionate, and strong. They often have great loads to bear but do so with God forever at their side.

Eve's story should always remind us of God's tremendous love for us. A love so deep that it brought the Son; His Son, who was able to, once and for all, forgive the transgressions of a remorseful human race.

In many interesting and varied ways Eve makes us take stock of ourselves. Eve makes us recognize our sinful nature and to keep God at the center of our lives. Eve enlightens us regarding our free will and the consequences of our actions. She is also a witness to the strength and capacity we have to be resilient in the most difficult of circumstances. She teaches us to be grateful and content, believing in God's anointing in our lives. Finally we learn from Eve that, regardless of our sins, God is both willing and longing to accept our penitence and embrace our return to Him.

Lord,

Like Eve, I, too, have made mistakes.

You know them as they weigh heavily upon my heart.

Stay with me as I remind myself that,
through Your Son, my sins have been forgiven.

Now I ask You to help me forgive myself.

Let me rejoice in Your love for me and move forward as
Your child, showing Your love to others in my words
and in my actions.

I ask this all in Christ's name
and with the guidance of the Holy Spirit.

Amen

The Word of God

Dear Friends, let us love one another, for love comes from God. Everyone who loves has been born of God and knows God, because God is love. *1 John 4:7-8*

If you remain in me and my words remain in you, ask for whatever you want and it will be done for you. *John 15:7*

When Jesus rose early on the first day of the week, he appeared first to Mary Magdalene, out of whom he had driven seven demons. She went and told those who had been with him and who were mourning and weeping. *Mark 16:9-10*

In the Lord, however, woman is not independent of man, nor is man independent of woman. For as woman came from man, so also man is born of woman. But everything comes from God. *1 Corinthians 11:11-12*

So God created man in his own image, in the image of God he created him; male and female he created them. *Genesis 1:27*

The Lord God said, "It is not good for the man to be alone. I will make a helper suitable for him. *Genesis 2:18*

Trust in the Lord with all your heart, on your own intelligence rely not; In all your ways be mindful of him, and he will make straight your paths. *Proverbs 3:5-6*

Freely Choosing God

Oftentimes it is difficult to separate our desires and longings from the Lord's will in our lives. Make a concentrated effort, every day this week, to ask the Lord to open the doors He would like you to go through and close all others. Have faith in His interest in your life and thank Him for what you know He will be doing. Let Him know that you put your life in His hands and trust in Him completely. Spend a few minutes, each day, in quiet meditation and record a few key thoughts when your session is over.

_____

_____

_____

_____

_____

_____

_____

_____

_____

_____

_____

_____

_____

_____

_____

_____

_____

_____

The biblical teaching taken as a whole enables us to say that predestination concerns all human persons, men and women, each and every one without exception

Mulieris Dignitatem

Noah's Wife

Sometimes, maybe even more often than we would like, our lot in life seems to be mundane but necessary. Day after day, week after week, we clean bathrooms, attend meetings, shop for groceries, do laundry, and carpool. Our lives are so full of chores that it seems as if we could be replaced by one well-oiled robot with decent driving skills. Yet we continue on with the belief that what we do makes a difference, and rightly so!

We find gratitude in the small things, the simple "thank-you's," and the occasional hug. It is our hope that from our tedium will arise treasures. We nurture our children, tend to our sick neighbor, and comfort our co-workers. We do these things for our family, our friends, and our neighbor knowing that caring for others is an edict from God. Deep inside we know the worth of our actions and trust in the value of what we do. We have a deep and unwavering faith in God's plan for our life. Part of that faith comes from learning others' stories and seeing how God worked in their lives.

Noah's wife and daughters-in-law are the heroines for the time in our life when we have to reach deep within ourselves and find joy where others might not. From Noah's wife, and her daughters-in-law, we clearly see how God is working miracles while she is taking care of the day-to-day necessities. Like us, there must have been times that these women wanted to give up, throw in the towel, and collapse from exhaustion. But they kept on working. Not because they were above reproach but because they were fulfilling God's purpose in their lives. God's design was energizing them just as it often energizes us. It gives us momentum when nothing else will. It is important for us to draw strength from the knowledge that our everyday lives, when truly lived for God's glory, never really have an ounce of tedium in them.

Whether we are loan officers, volunteer clinicians, restaurant workers, CEOs, or full-time mothers we can never underestimate what we bring to others in our daily living. Just as important is the realization that it is the commitment to our everyday tasks that allow us to develop the perseverance required to be disciples of Christ. From that foundation of tenacity Christ will be able to bring our lives into fruition and blessed beyond imagination.

If we are not finding joy in our everyday lives and able to give gratitude for what we currently have, we cannot ask to move ahead and acquire more. It is to our benefit to work diligently, for God's glory, in whatever circumstances He has put us while we thank Him, and believe in His word, for the blessings that are unfolding. Just as Noah's wife was assiduously working to make the ark's mission a success, so were untold blessings unfolding for the future of mankind: namely its survival.

We find renewal in the understanding that, when we are working with God, our journey will be enriched by a wide variety of people and circumstances in which we are both givers and takers. We do not see what God has in store but should put our complete faith and trust in Him.

Had she known what lie ahead, what might Noah's wife's reaction have been at the outset of the journey? Like most of us, she must have seen her own weaknesses and probably would have abandoned the idea that she could be of help. If she had heard the weather forecasts with the tremendous torrential rains and seen video clips of the animals in their stalls, she might have run in the opposite direction. Perhaps this is why God wisely withholds so much from us. Nonetheless, there she was on the ark. And, just as God would hope, she worked diligently to bring about the success of God's plan.

Do we work just as diligently knowing that we are all part of God's plan for the earth? Is He waiting for us to show Him our tenacity before His blessings become known? While we do not know the answer to this, we do know that the traits of diligence and perseverance are highly revered in Scripture.

In Scripture we learn about these women and yet never know their names. Indeed, their names could be our names and our names could be theirs. These incredible women lent the physical and emotional support needed to attain victory for the Ark's purpose. As women, we know, or can certainly imagine, what had to be accomplished on that expedition. Laundry, toilets, and meals come quickly to mind. Add in the captivity, along with the animals, and we can all shake our heads in agreement, "Yes, we know what these women went through."

But so it was that from their tedium God saved humankind from extinction. From the monotony of their endless days caring for a multitude of animals and the daily needs of the people on the ark, these women ushered in the most beautiful of treasures. They help us realize that our daily tasks happen amidst many of God's miracles. They ushered in the continued existence of humanity. And yet we never learn their names. How might our existence mirror theirs? Let us look for the miracles that are happening all around us and thank God for them.

We can picture how these women would have worked tirelessly, side-by-side, with their spouses. Like us, they would have worked with a gratitude that could only come from understanding the innate value of what was being done. They would have, even in their exhaustion, found time for prayer and thanksgiving to the God who cared for them, the God we now serve and worship. This is the same loving God who set us upon our current path and associated us with our current friends and family. He is our tender God. He is our exacting Father.

Indeed, God's demands are very clear when we consider how arduous these women's lives must have been. We can understand His conditions when we consider that even with His concern for their survival, how much was required of them. It is the same with us. As we read in Ecclesiastes 3:2-8, we are reminded that our lives, too, will be filled with a variety of seasons. God gives each season, whether it is the time for weeping or the time for laughter, to us. And so, in looking to Noah's wife and daughters-in-law we can recognize these different seasons and know their necessity in God's plan. We can look to these women and understand that the seasons of our lives are a necessary part of our own survival, growth, and spiritual awakening.

Like these women, God cares for our physical survival and spiritual growth. However, for both of these to occur, we need to work persistently with Him, just as Noah's wife and daughters-in-law did. And in so doing we, too, must often find joy in the mundane. We, too, must look to a God who loves us immensely and find both our comfort and our peace in that knowledge. Whether it is our time to mourn or our time to dance, we must find solace in each season knowing that God is with us. He is a strong shoulder to cry on or a wonderful dance partner.

But how do we respond to God during the different seasons of our life? Do we remember that He has a bigger plan for us that we may not see? Do we work joyfully and persistently knowing that, in doing so, we glorify Him? Do we continue to love and worship Him through all the times of our life? Do we remember how important our work is even if we, too, forever remain nameless?

It is vital for us to remember that our contribution is no less valuable because of our anonymity. The world values notoriety and fame. God values our focus on Him and His call in our life. When we fully live and breathe for God, our life, and what we offer up with it, is as important as Noah's wife's life and the lives of his daughters-in-law. As wives, mothers, and cherished friends, our lives take on a new meaning when we look to these nameless, faceless, and yet ultimately amazing women for a renewed understanding of the treasure in our everyday tasks.

Lord,

Let me always remember that You have a plan for me
that is greater than I could ever imagine.

Let that understanding be my guide as I care for those
you have put into my life and reach out to those whose lives
I might touch.

Let me always remember that serving others is a way to
serve You and that loving others is a way to love You.

Let my anonymity, whether it be for a season
or a lifetime, be for Your glory.

Let me live for You all the days of my life.

Amen

The Word of God

There is a time for everything, and a season for every
activity under heaven:

A time to be born and a time to die,
A time to plant and a time to uproot,
A time to kill and a time to heal,
A time to tear down and a time to build,
A time to weep and a time to laugh,
A time to mourn and a time to dance,
A timer to scatter stones and a time to gather them,
A time to embrace and a time to refrain, a time to keep
and a time to throw away,
A time to tear and a time to mend, a time to be silent and a
time to speak,
A time to love and a time to hate,
A time for war and a time for peace.

Ecclesiastes 3:1-8

I know what it is to be in need, and I know what it is to
have plenty. I have learned the secret of being content in
any and every situation, whether well fed or hungry,
whether living in plenty or in want. I can do everything
through him who gives me strength. Philippians 4:12-13

I know that there is nothing better for men than to be happy and do good while they live. That everyone may eat and drink and find satisfaction in all his toil-this is the gift of God. Ecclesiastes 3:12-13

Do everything without grumbling or questioning, that you may be blameless and innocent, children of God without blemish in the midst of a crooked and perverse generation, among whom you shine like lights in the world, as you hold on to the world of life, so that my boast for the day of Christ may be that I did not run in vain or labor in vain. Philippians 2:14-16

Serving Others

Your daily routine should now feel more fully immersed in the Lord than ever before. You begin and end each day with an affirmation statement steeped in your innate worth in Christ. You look for and welcome opportunities to be led by the Holy Spirit. You spend a few minutes, or more, each day meditating on God's word and in solitude with Him. You are now ready to move outside of yourself for this week's task...

This week you will find a way to serve others, anonymously, for the Glory of God. Consider giving an hour or two to a local nursing home, a hospice organization, a pregnancy help center, or in some other capacity that the Lord is calling you. Let the Lord speak to you, through His Spirit, and fulfill this call both joyously and graciously.

Jesus' attitude to the women whom he meets in the course of his Messianic service reflects the eternal plan of God, who, in creating each one of them, chooses her and loves her in Christ.

Mulieris Dignitatem

Sarah

We are first introduced to Sarah in Genesis 11:29. Here we know her as Sarai, wife of Abram and daughter-in-law of Terah. Throughout the Genesis story we understand that Sarah is quite beautiful and seems to be a typical wife with longings to be a mother. It is important to understand that the physical attribute of beauty, in the Old Testament, is also a statement of righteousness, virtue, and often spiritual prowess. For Sarah these characteristics are evidenced by her role in the conversion of hundreds, maybe thousands, of people from pagan beliefs to monotheism as well as the fact that her tent was literally and figuratively open to all; welcoming and providing sustenance to any who were in need. She was a virtuous woman of God.

As the Genesis story progresses however, we learn that Sarah is barren. This becomes the focus of her existence as her longing for children continues to be unmet. Indeed, in the

Scripture verse that lets us know of Sarah's barrenness, it also follows with an interesting four words: she had no children. This becomes a stark contrast to her other, godly characteristics and yet may also be fueled by her own husband's pursuit of the same thing: an heir to all he has been blessed with, through his own seed.

So, while in one way this double defined account (barren/had no children) looks like clarification on the statement regarding Sarah's childlessness, in another way this looks like two different statements. In fact, the more we come to know Sarah, we can see that her treatment of Hagar, her maidservant, is seemingly without compassion, thus making her "barren" in an emotional sense. We see Sarah's complexity just as easily as we may see our own.

Soon, we even come to see Sarah's barrenness as a driving force in both her marriage and her treatment of others. Yet it is easy for us to sympathize with her and her situation. We are easily able to recall the times in our life when particular goals or interests have single-mindedly driven us forward.

Not only might Sarah remind us of ourselves and the barren times in our life, but she is also our mother in faith. It is from her lineage that we are able to trace ourselves back to Abraham and God's covenant. She will become the mother of the countless descendants that God promises Abraham. We will learn her story and witness how no one could replace her in this promise. And in that way, she is our foster mother, as we trace our faith back to the worship of the one true God, father of Jesus, triune with the Holy Spirit.

In Sarah we have a heroine who displays love, joy, doubt, jealousy and impatience. She is so very real and so very much like us. Recall that God promises Abram that Sarah will conceive, even though she is far past her childbearing years. Given her age, Sarah laughs at this promise from God.

However, God is not offended by her reaction and we see His loving kindness as He fulfills His promise. The entire chain of events is meant to show us that nothing is ever too big, too far-fetched for God.

Sarah has a life filled with working with the Spirit of God and yet experiences a "barrenness" and her faith waivers. We are duty bound to recall that she was considered, along with Abraham, to be a great converter of pagan people to the monotheistic religion of Judaism. Sarah also showed tremendous trust in God when she followed Abraham as he responded to God's call to "Go forth from the land of your kinsfolk and from your father's house to a land I will show you." Indeed, throughout her life she put her faith in God in a way that we are all called to do but still had those times where her faith wasn't enough. Don't we all experience those droughts when our resolve seems to dissipate in the face of a particularly daunting challenge or in our own selfish interests to blindly pursue a desire that we harbor in the depths of our hearts? So it was for Sarah as she longed to have a child. Those longings took hold of her and shook her faith in God. And yet He remained faithful to her!

In that way, Sarah helps us learn two very important aspects of God. First, the understanding that nothing is too tremendous, too austere for God. Second, that God never forgets His promises. But we see that Sarah both doubts and laughs at the prospect of God's promises, even after she has taken such an active role in bringing the knowledge of a monotheistic God to a pagan nation. Like us, Sarah is multifaceted. Don't we have times where we can feel our lives very much in sync with the Spirit and, paradoxically, experience times when we are filled with fear or jealousy or an emotion that really has no place if we fully trust in God?

How often do we, like Sarah, doubt that God will be true to us or true to His word? How often have we lost our focus on what is set in Scripture and, instead, put it on what is set in the secular world? How often do we find ourselves being impatient in our circumstances instead of believing that we are right where God wants us to be? And finally, how often has our great and loving God forgiven us when we display the non-Christian characteristics of jealousy, resentment, and doubt?

As we read Sarah's story we know that she should hold out for the Lord's plan to unfold, but that is because we are privy to the ending. We know she will bear a son, just as God promised.

Sarah, however, being impatient and unable to wait for God's plan to unfold, insists that Abraham have relations with her maid Hagar. And, as a result of these relations, Hagar gives birth to Ishmael. Sarah's plan to bring children into Abraham's life seems to backfire, as Hagar appears to be boisterous at this new position in the household. Indeed, no one is pleased with the results of this plan. Abraham still cries out to God for an heir of his own seed and Sarah soon finds herself being taunted by Hagar in a way that undermines her own role as woman of the house, so to speak. Neither Sarah nor Abraham find resolve in the consequences of an action they took upon themselves to initiate.

It makes us ask ourselves: How often have we formulated the best of plans only to see them unfold in a less than desirable way? How often have we, like Sarah, moved ahead and not held out for the Lord's plan to evolve in His own time?

When our own self-interests are placed before God's will, we jeopardize our life's purpose. Driven by our own desires only serves to separate us from God. This is why time spent in prayer, meditation, and studying Scripture allows us a deeper fellowship with our creator. These things promulgate a rich, more personal relationship with God. From this point we are then able to live according to His edicts.

But like Sarah, we can most certainly think of countless times when our own excitement and anticipation cloud our decisions. We plow ahead with our own ideas and expectations. Probably more often than we know, our impatience has diminished the plans that the Lord has had in store for us. In learning about Sarah's journey (both physical and emotional) we are able to learn how we add both time and frustration to the events of our lives when we put our own interests before the Lord's interests.

Indeed, as Christian women, we can take so much from Sarah's story. We learn about God's commitment to us and His faithfulness to His covenant. In the end we witness His loving kindness in such a way that we ought to feel quite indebted. However all He really wants is our love, freely given.

There is simply no way for us to repay our Lord for all He does in our lives other than to use our free will in accepting and returning His unconditional love: the unconditional love so beautifully given to us in Jesus Christ. No debt is ever easier to repay than our debt to God through the acceptance of Jesus Christ.

Sarah's story shows us, in no uncertain terms, that our own focus can fog our vision of what really matters: trusting God. And yet, like Eve, Sarah's story tells of the Lord's commitment to His word even when we do our best to jeopardize things. God so loves Sarah that He never forsakes her and we have that same place in His heart.

Consider the fact that even when Sarah scoffs at the idea that God will grant her a child in her old age, God is not put off. Indeed, the God we serve is always faithful to His declarations. And so Sarah gives birth to Isaac when she is ninety years old. The more we learn about God the more we will see that it makes perfect sense for Sarah to give birth at this very old age. In this, she cannot give credit to anyone other than God. At ninety years old, and with Abraham one hundred years old, we can be certain that Isaac's birth is a gift from God. We say this with an understanding that God's hand was fully part of this and not just as an esoteric remark. Make no mistakes about it, Sarah giving birth at ninety requires us to give all credit to God.

In the meantime, Abram and Hagar's son, Ishmael, was growing up. Remember that Ishmael had been born to Abram and Hagar when Sarah's impatience had gotten the better of her. Convinced that she would never have children, she encouraged Abram to have relations with her maid, Hagar. Now, for Sarah, the bitterness of this reminder of Abraham's other son, from a different woman, was too much for her to bear. Filled with jealousy she orders Abraham to *"Get rid of that slave woman and her son, for the slave woman's son will never share in the inheritance with my son Isaac." Genesis 21:10b*

However, this chain of events with Sarah and Hagar must happen so that God's ultimate promise may come to be. God had made a covenant with Abraham and told him that he would be the father of many nations. That would happen with Sarah and not Hagar.

Nonetheless, we shudder at the realization that Sarah's original interference in God's plan brought about this climactic result to Hagar and her son. Had Sarah had the patience and faith that what God promised would come to be, then she would not have asked Abraham to have relations with Hagar. And, of course, the ensuing jealousy would have not taken place.

In our life we undoubtedly cause trouble or sadness to others. Whether through our own greed, impatience, or thoughtlessness we have certainly been the cause of pain or anguish. We are probably aware of most of these occasions as they happen or very shortly thereafter. Hopefully, as we get older we are developing a compassion towards others that diminishes our capacity to inflict such unkindness. We become aware of how our actions affect other people.

On the other hand, Sarah's story gives us insight into the times where our actions cause pain and we remain unaware. She makes us take note of those remorseful times, which may very well be revealed to us at the end of our life, when the knowledge of how we have hurt or saddened others is beyond remedy. Our awareness of the error of Sarah's mistreatment of Hagar should be reflected in our daily life as we act more conscientiously in words and deeds.

We must also see the irony that, even after God gave Sarah all she had ever dreamed about, a son, she still finds jealousy and rage in her heart. Again we ask ourselves, how many times have we been in that same situation? Our lives are working well: we have our health, our family, and our friends. We have food to eat and share laughter with others. And still, envy has a way of making itself known in our lives. So it is that Sarah again shows us that even when God keeps His word and blesses our lives, we are sometimes less than grateful. We, too, find ourselves forgetting to look at what we have and choosing to focus on what we don't have.

In fact, Sarah's life was changed so much that God changed her name as well. Sarai became Sarah. Abram became Abraham. We, too, have most certainly experienced those life-changing moments. They might come in the form of the birth of a child, a near fatal accident, or the acquisition of a new and rewarding opportunity. We want to move forward, feel ready to forge ahead, and yet find some of our old "selves" still surfacing. So it was with Sarah. Regardless of her good fortune she still experiences a jealousy towards Hagar. She still exhibits such unkindness towards Hagar that an angel of the Lord must reassure Hagar that she is being heard.

In Sarah's response to Hagar and Ishmael, we are reminded that Sarah's barrenness does seem to go beyond her ability to have children. Sarah's barrenness appears to include her inability to show compassion and kindness towards Hagar and Ishmael. She allows us to meditate on the barrenness in our lives and know that, even in the driest of times, God is with us. Sarah forces us to ask ourselves difficult questions: How often are our emotions barren? In what circumstances is jealousy or impatience driving our decisions? And in these situations, how can we return to God and His caring arms? Although we are on our own sovereign journeys, our paths are continuously crossed with others' paths. How we interact and influence others will speak of our love for Jesus. Being part of a community provides opportunity for us to develop a loving and compassionate attitude towards all people.

In Scripture we are told that how we treat others is how we are treating Jesus. Jesus asks us how we would be able to love a God that we cannot see when we can't even love the people that we can see. Sarah reminds us of this dilemma.

Clearly we serve a God whose love is so absolute that even in our ungratefulness it cannot be diminished. Sarah assists us in attaining the full realization that God's love is unconditional regardless of our "humanness." Sarah's life resounds with beauty for us because she is so very real, so very temporal, and so very blessed by God. There is great comfort in the knowledge that even in our most transient of moments, our God never abandons us.

Sarah, then, prods us to stay the course with God. She teaches us the value of patience and the need for loving-kindness to others. Her story resounds with the knowledge that, even if we try to altar or direct circumstances, no one can take our place in God's plan. Hagar simply could not replace Sarah in God's plan and promise to Abraham. But God would not abandon Hagar either. She also became part of the plan.

Like Sarah, each and every one of us has a role to fill for God. We have no need to let jealousy or envy occupy our thoughts. Those emotions speak of a belief that God's love and blessings are finite when in fact they are infinite. Sarah never needed to be jealous of Hagar because God had enough love and anointings for both their lives. Just as He has enough, right now, to shower each and every one of us with blessings beyond compare.

In the end, we see that her life changes in ways so great that God changes her name as well. Sarai becomes Sarah. She is reborn in Him just as we are reborn in Christ. A beautiful moment indeed: both for Sarah and for ourselves. Through Sarah we are reminded of God's great love for us and how He will always be true to His commitment. In this knowledge, we are given all the more reason to study and learn His edicts, His ways.

When we understand how to work with Him and the Holy Spirit, our lives become filled with purpose. We live, then, as we ought to live: for Him and His glory. We do well when we remind ourselves that the word of God remains as true today, as beautiful today, as it was thousands of years ago. He remains as true to us as He was to Sarah.

Lord,

When I forget the depth of Your love for me,
let me be reminded of it in new and deeper ways.

When I forget Your faithfulness to Your word,
let me be reminded of it in new and deeper ways.

When I forget my obligations to You,
let me be reminded of them in new and deeper ways.

May my love for You continue to grow,
daily, in new and deeper ways

and when my time on earth is complete
may I be welcomed into Your loving arms
and know that I am where I belong.

Amen

The Word of God

God also said to Abraham, "As for Sarai your wife, you are no longer to call her Sarai; her name will be Sarah. I will bless her and will surely give you a son by her. I will bless her so that she will be the mother of nations; kings of people will come from her. *Genesis 17:15-16*

Remember this: Whoever sows sparingly will also reap sparingly, and whoever sows generously will also reap generously. *2 Corinthians 9:6*

In your anger do not sin. Do not let the sun go down while you are still angry, and do not give the devil a foothold. *Ephesians 4:26-27*

The matter distressed Abraham greatly because it concerned his son. But God said to him, "Do not be so distressed about the boy and your maid-servant. Listen to whatever Sarah tells you, because it is through Isaac that your offspring will be reckoned. I will make the son of the maidservant into a nation also, because he is your offspring. *Genesis 21:11-13*

Now the Lord was gracious to Sarah, as he had said, and the Lord did for Sarah what he had promised. Sarah became pregnant and bore a son to Abraham in his old age, at the very time God had promised him. *Genesis 21: 1-2*

Replacing Jealousy or Impatience with Gratitude

Throughout the course of a day we may find times where our feelings turn to jealousy, impatience, or envy. This week you will be on your guard against these emotions so that you may thoughtfully and purposely begin replacing them with feelings of joy and gratitude.

Find at least three different instances this week where your inclination is be impatient or jealous. Then, in these situations, recall that God blesses you in His own time and in His own way. Find a way to be grateful for this knowledge. This doesn't mean to be grateful at someone else's misfortune but to be appreciative in how the Lord is already working in your life.

Use the following page to make a simple recording of each instance where you are able to turn your impatience or jealousy into gratitude. Even when the week is over, make an effort to live with a more grateful, joyful attitude. The rewards will be tremendous!

One

_____
_____
_____
_____
_____
_____
_____

Two

_____
_____
_____
_____
_____
_____
_____

Three

_____
_____
_____
_____
_____
_____
_____

All of God's action in human history at all times respects the free will of the human "I."

Mulieris Dignitatem

Lot's Wife

The genealogy in Scripture is both fascinating and a bit confusing for those of us not considered biblical scholars. For instance, most of us know the story of Lot but do not know that Lot was Abraham's nephew. Lot's father, Haran, was Abraham's brother. Or we may recall that Lot's wife was turned to a pillar of salt but not know that Lot was quite wealthy when he and Abraham went their separate ways: with Lot settling near the city of Sodom.

What we know about Lot's wife is little indeed and yet what we can learn from her is immense. Here is a woman whose family lives in a city where debauchery, greed, and licentiousness are prevalent. Essentially, Sodom could represent any fair city today that is operating outside of God's laws. It might be my city, it might be your city. So, like Lot's wife, many of us probably live within cities that are an affront to the Lord.

And, like Lot's wife, we have come to know and cherish our lives within these cities. We may watch the news and be appalled by the happenings within our city limits but, for the most part, tend to continue living in our cities. We would be hard pressed to move or to imagine ourselves elsewhere. Where we live is a part of who we are and creates the fabric of our existence. We seek out the good and try to remedy or disregard the bad.

It would seem fair to assume that Lot's wife had the same kind of feelings towards her city and home that we have about our cities and our homes. She saw the worthy and tried to disregard the wicked. Even when she was led from her city by an angel of God and told not to look back, her sadness, regret, or even curiosity got the better of her.

Imagine what her reaction would have been when she learned she had to leave her city, her home. It would have been only human to feel opposition to such an idea. We have all read countless stories of people who refused to be evacuated, who choose to take their chances against impending doom: whether it be from hurricanes, floods, tornadoes, or volcanoes. Maybe Lot's wife was like that. Like most people in the same situation, she probably left grudgingly, unwillingly. And, in her grief, made the fatal mistake to look back at what she was leaving.

Our lives are packed with the same predicament: God tries to move us forward but we keep looking back. Although the idea of looking back so that we are able to move forward in a positive way is certainly commendable, for the most part we tend to look back unproductively. And, like Lot's wife, our lives are often in ruins because of this instinct, this longing, this habit to look over our shoulder at what "was." Like

Peter, who loses his footing when he takes his eyes off Jesus, we, too, lose our way when we take our eyes off God. Our eyes should stay fixed on God who is doing His very best to save us, often from ourselves.

We should not be surprised that God will always do what He has to do in order to deliver us from impending disaster. What should surprise us is how often He will try, given our stubbornness to attempt to do things our way and to settle things according to our will. Haven't we all faced circumstances that we would prefer to avoid, believing our knowledge was the ultimate knowledge and our plan the better plan? Isn't there a time when life has made us move in one direction when we would have preferred another? But when we are living for God we can trust His word that all things will work for His good. With that knowledge, that trust, comes our ability to be led by His Spirit into new and uncharted territories.

When we trust God we are able to move in those intimidating times. In His love our fears do not immobilize us. With our confidence placed firmly in Him we are able to let go of the past, knowing that all it held has brought us to this place with Him, right here, right now. We must always believe in His providence and have faith in His ultimate love for us. And so, when guided by the Spirit, we progress, we forge ahead. And, like Lot's wife, we are better to leave the past behind. We need to keep our eye on the future and our focus on God.

But do we look back? Of course we do. And don't these glimpses of the past haunt us? They most certainly do. But Lot's wife is here to remind us, in no uncertain terms, that the past is just that: past. The purpose of our past is that we learn from it but that we also be willing to give it over to God when it is too much to bear. In that way we are able to be most fully alive in the present, which is truly a gift from God.

Did Lot's wife suffer the ultimate consequences for that brief glimpse of what she was leaving behind? She did. And don't we, when we nurture that part of ourselves that finds comfort in our own sorrows, or our own martyrdoms, also suffer consequences? We absolutely do. Are they the ultimate consequences? They are in that they keep us from living for God's glory in the here and now. They hinder us from the joy that God has in mind for our lives. And in that way, they continually alter our relationship with God.

Consider the time we spend nursing old wounds as if our very life depended on them. Too often we use them as excuses for our current dilemmas. We don't want to learn from them but prefer to lean on them. We nurture them, tend to them, and stash them away for a rainy day. We don't allow them to die for fear we will need them. We allow them to fester until they become ailments in our physical bodies. We allow those wounds, instead of the Holy Spirit, to take hold of us and lead our tomorrows. Too much of the time that should be given to God, and to the people He has brought into our lives, is spent in idle pity or in sorrow for what might have been or what will never be.

Does this mean we shouldn't allow ourselves to rightfully mourn certain things in our lives? Of course it doesn't. There are volumes of works published on the healing characteristics of forgiveness. Let us remind ourselves that Jesus came for those of us who need His healing, whether physical or emotional. It would be foolish for us to abandon this offering.

Indeed, we should turn over our repentant or saddened hearts to Him. We should learn from our past experiences, whether perpetuated by us or upon us, and create a better future for ourselves through Christ. We should also loosen our grip on our old wounds. Let us enjoin our tragedies and sadness with the death of Jesus on the cross. And in so doing, we place these things at Christ's feet where they might be washed away in the blood and water of His wounds.

This allows us, then, a starting point, our own earthly resurrection, in which we will be able to enjoy God's gift of life and friendship in new and deeper ways. And as those wounds resurface, because they most assuredly will, we continually give them over to Jesus. In that way we show, through our words and our spiritual actions, our complete trust in Him.

As often happens, the Old Testament foreshadows messages in the New Testament. We might consider the message of Lot's wife, with its dire consequences, to be a forerunner to the simple but succinct verse regarding Simon's mother-in-law. That same message of "letting go and moving on" is made rather quickly in Luke 4:38-39.

Jesus left the synagogue and went to the home of Simon. Now Simon's mother-in-law was suffering from a high fever, and they asked Jesus to help her. So he bent over her and rebuked the fever, and it left her. She got up at once and began to wait on them.

We don't read that they all sat around and marveled at what had just happened. Simon's mother-in-law didn't go on and on about her near death experience. In fact, it is quite telling that there were no reactions whatsoever. Indeed, the faith of those who asked Jesus for His help was such that they simply knew it would be forthcoming and successful. Business was at hand. It, once again, shows us the reciprocal nature of our relationship with Christ. On the one hand He **does** for us so that we can **do** for others. On the other hand when we **do** for others we open the floodgates for Him to **do** for us. It becomes all about "doing," about action. When the faith in our heart is so incredibly strong, love and compassion drive our actions. It is as if we can't do enough for others because our love for Jesus, and seeing Him in everyone, propels us forward. We pray for others, we counsel others, we help one another, and we show compassion and mercy. We live for Christ in the purest of ways. We don't lose our todays to our yesterdays. We become thankful for what the past held and what we learned from it and then express gratitude for a new day to glorify the Lord.

Simon's mother-in-law shows us, like Lot's wife, that our goal is to move forward to do the work of Jesus, whatever that might entail. For her, it was caring for those around her. For us it might be the same but in a different capacity; maybe as a supervisor or as a colleague. However, we live in a secular world that gives us a message that is in direct opposition to the message in Scripture. We are often encouraged to win-at-all-costs or to accept callousness as a "life lesson." Through scripture passages, however, we are encouraged to take the spotlight off of ourselves and shine it on others who might benefit from our care, our time, and our focus. We can surely count on God's Word that in that way we are ultimately helping ourselves. He knows what works!

Lot's wife, just like Simon's mother-in-law, prods us to let our yesterdays go. She reminds us that, in looking back, we sacrifice the future. A future meant for God. Without ambiguity, Lot's wife forces our focus ahead, leaving what should be behind us, behind us. Combined with Jesus' death on the cross, we should allow the pain or sadness from our yesterdays to be washed away in His blood. We then can eagerly anticipate each day as a chance to live in the joy and peace that Jesus gave us through His death and resurrection.

Lord,

You work all things for Your good.

May all my yesterdays serve Your purpose
and work together to bring me always to You.

May my focus today be on You and Your will in my
life.

May all my todays belong only to You.

I give You praise and thanksgiving for this day.

My faith is placed firmly in You as I open my heart to
the guidance of the Holy Spirit.

May all my works give glory to You
and in all ways serve Your greater good.

Amen

The Word of God

But Jesus told him, "Follow me, and let the dead bury their own dead." *Matthew 8:22*

No one who puts his hand to the plow and looks back is fit for service in the kingdom of God. *Luke 9:62*

Cast all your anxiety on him because he cares for you. *1 Peter 5:7*

We wait in hope for the Lord; he is our help and our shield. In him our hearts rejoice, for we trust in his holy name. *Psalm 33:20-21*

Then the Lord rained down burning sulfur on Sodom and Gomorrah-from the Lord out of the heavens. Thus he overthrew those cities and the entire plain, including all those living in the cities-and also the vegetation in the land. But Lot's wife looked back, and she became a pillar of salt. *Genesis 19:24-26*

Forget the former things; do not dwell on the past. See, I am doing a new thing! Now it springs up; do you not perceive it? *Isaiah 43:18-19*

Letting Go

For the past few weeks you have been engaged in nurturing your relationship with God in ways that allow you to be all He wants you to be. You have written an affirmation statement based on your tremendous worth in Christ and have invited the Holy Spirit to guide you, work with you, and lead you to God. You have worked in an anonymous way to help others and have given a few minutes a day to meditating on God's word. It is now time to another dimension to your personal journey...

Brainstorm a list of adjectives that describe feelings you know you must now give over to God in order to continue on your journey. Ask God to show you what you must now turn over to Him. They are roadblocks that are ready to be torn down. During your next quiet time with God, read your list to Him. Ask Him for deliverance from these impediments. Prayerfully trust in Him.

_____

_____

_____

_____

_____

_____

_____

_____

_____

_____

Thus in the same context as the creation of man and woman, the biblical account speaks of God's instituting marriage as an indispensable condition for the transmission of life to new generations, the transmission of life to which marriage and conjugal love are by their nature ordered: "Be fruitful and multiply, and fill the earth and subdue it."

Mulieris Dignitatem

Rebekah

Rebekah is Sarah's daughter-in-law. She married Sarah's beloved son, Isaac. When we read Genesis we can't help but notice that there are many similarities between Sarah and Rebekah. Additionally, we know that as the wife of Isaac, it is with Rebekah that the Lord will continue delivering His promise. The covenant He made with Abraham that his descendents would be more numerous than the stars in the sky will proceed with Rebekah as Isaac's wife.

Rebekah's story actually begins with Abraham's search for a wife for his son, Isaac. In his old age Abraham sent his chief servant on this mission. Abraham made his servant promise to go back to the land of Abraham's relatives. Abraham did not want his servant to find a wife from among the Canaanite women. Abraham's allegiance was with the God of his ancestors: our God, the one true God. And so his servant went, with as much trust in Abraham as Abraham had in God.

For her part we have to assume that Rebekah was also a trusting and allegiant young woman. We are able to marvel at how easily God's plan unfolded for her. She shows us how God is always in even the small details of our lives. Here we have a number of young women going to a well to draw water right at the moment that Abraham's servant is at the well. We hear the servant asking the God of Abraham to make it clear if any of the women at the well is called to be the one for whom he was sent.

Rebekah is that woman. She has many traits that make her the fulfillment of God's plan for His people. Rebekah is filled with compassion, strength, and loving-kindness; often called *chesed*. Rebekah is from the family necessary to be a suitable wife for Isaac but also must willingly accept the marriage offer. Her father is Nahor, Abraham's brother. The entire scene at the well which prepares us to join Rebekah's journey towards Isaac and to take her place in the line of Jewish Matriarchs is one filled with anticipation and excitement.

Rebekah's traits of compassion, strength, and chesed are witnessed by her offer of water to both Abraham's servant but also in offering water for his camels. This is no easy task to be accomplished and takes the combination of all three traits to be successful. Her compassion and chesed would have been the impetus for her to make these offers to the stranger and her strength would have allowed her to work the well in such a way as to supply water to camels who are known to hold tremendous amounts of the liquid, thus requiring an arduous commitment on Rebekah's part to fill.

Recall, also, that Abraham sent his servant in complete faith that God would guide the journey. Abraham's servant had that same complete faith in Abraham, and subsequently Abraham's God. Rebekah must also have had the same faith as she listened to the servant's story of his assignment and accepted the proposal. This total faith in God is shown to us, over and over again, throughout Scripture. Faith, we read, heals. Faith, we learn, moves mountains. Faith, we witness, brings salvation.

Throughout the story we see that there are numerous ways in which Isaac and Rebekah's life mirrors Abraham and Sarah's. As well as being barren like Sarah, the beautiful Rebekah was the cause of a lie that Isaac felt he had to make regarding Rebekah's identity when they were in the foreign land of Gerar. In Gerar, Isaac tells the men that Rebekah is his sister. He does this because he believes that the men might kill him to have Rebekah, should they know that Rebekah is his wife. Not until the king of the Philistines, Abimelech, sees Isaac caressing Rebekah is their lie uncovered. At this point the king orders that both Isaac and Rebekah should remain untouched and unharmed. To make himself clear the king announces that anyone disobeying this order would be put to death. This is quite similar to Abraham's lie regarding Sarah's identity when they were in Egypt (Genesis 12:10-20). Ultimately, like Sarah before her, Rebekah's presence in a foreign land becomes the reason for safe passage and the eventual fulfillment of God's plan.

It is an interesting statement that the beauty of each woman was, at first, cause for concern on her husband's part, and then became the reason for their safe existence in an alien environment.

It was a woman whose existence ushered in protection for God's plan to continue to manifest. It was imperative that Rebekah's offspring, in lineage with Sarah, inherit the promise of great blessings from God. Once again, we are reminded that each one of us has a unique calling that no one else can fill. Each of us, whether we remain anonymous or draw fame, is an active part of God's plan. If we do not fulfill our purpose, no one else will. And so, these women who are our ancestors in faith, remind us to stay true to God knowing and believing that He is working in our lives.

Not only was Rebekah, like Sarah, considered to be quite beautiful but she was also barren. So, as did his father before him, Isaac *prayed to the Lord on behalf of his wife, because she was barren (Genesis 25:21).*

Rebekah's circumstances, like Sarah's, give us a powerful example of intercessory prayer. While our personal relationship with Jesus allows us to turn to Him with our joy, our sadness, and our hopes there are also times when we should heed the value of intercession. There are times that our supplications, along with others' on our behalf, become powerful indeed. And, of course, the reverse is true. We should understand the need and triumphant nature of our intercession for others. So, when Isaac prays to the Lord to open Rebekah's womb, we see first hand the intrinsic value of intercessory prayer. Along with feeding the hungry and clothing the naked we should always understand the value of praying for others. In that way we are raising each other to the Lord, for His care and His mercy.

As a result of Isaac's prayer, Rebekah becomes pregnant with twins. As events unfold we find that these twins, Jacob and Esau, develop very different personalities: Esau, the first born, becomes a skillful hunter while Jacob, the second born, grows into a quiet, somewhat reflective man. As young men we learn that these very diverse personalities each draw a different parent into favoritism. Rebekah favors Jacob while Isaac favors Esau.

When we next encounter Rebekah, her children are grown. She is eavesdropping on a conversation that Esau is having with Isaac. Isaac is instructing Esau to go and hunt some wild game and prepare it for Isaac. Isaac wants to enjoy the meal and give Esau his blessing. Isaac knows that he is nearing the end of his life and wants to put his estate in order, so to speak. This includes giving Esau the blessing customarily meant for the first born. Isaac wants to make sure he does this before he dies.

Because Rebekah favors Jacob, she intentionally undermines the blessing that Isaac intended for Esau. In doing this she ensures that Jacob inherits the sanctification intended for Esau. Rebekah devises a ruse in which Jacob misleads his father into believing that he is Esau (as Isaac is too old to see) and subsequently "steals" Esau's blessing. Whether we agree with her tactics or not, most mothers are able to understand the need to provide extra protection to that one child we see as "vulnerable" or "needy." From that perspective it seems impossible not to understand her actions.

Jewish teachings on Rebekah also add a depth to the understanding of this matriarch. According to many such writings, Rebekah understood that Jacob was more spiritually attuned than Esau and would, therefore, be able to most completely fulfill the role that God had ordained for the lineage of Abraham. She saw that her hand was needed in directing the outcome of the situation. God must have counted on her and in that way His will was done.

Rebekah, then, very clearly shows us the two sides of ourselves. Both that side that is able to work with the Holy Spirit and accept the path that we are on as well as the side that is able to take matters into our own hands. Rebekah's story encourages us to prayerfully move through our lives, learning the word of God and developing a deep, passionate relationship with Jesus. And in so doing, know that we are to be ever watchful of our steps and yet trusting that they are in sync with our Creator when we ask Him to lead the way.

Rebekah gives us a beautiful example of that trust when she accepts Abraham's servant's offer at the well. She then shows us her "lioness" instincts as a mother when she intervenes on Isaac's behalf. Certainly, after contemplating the entire story of Esau and Jacob, we can assume that God chose Rebekah because He could count on her ability to determine the times to react and the times to accept. Rebekah is our beautiful example of working with God.

In the New Testament, Rebekah's skill at reading and knowing how to work with God is reiterated in the story of Mary and Martha (Luke 10:38-41). Both women are in the company of Jesus. Mary sits at His feet, understanding her call at that moment. Martha, on the other hand, busies herself. She is most certainly preparing food and drink. As Martha complains to Jesus that Mary is not being helpful, Jesus quickly says that it is Mary who is reacting correctly in the given circumstances. So here we have two women in the exact same moment in time but with different responses. The story very clearly shows us that our walk with God requires our understanding of each step along the way. When we continue to develop our relationship with Him, through prayer, anointed friendships, and learning His word, we are more apt to make the right choices, like Mary, in our day-to-day lives.

We look to these women: Rebekah, Mary, and Martha to gain insight into knowing God and following His Spirit. We see the value of loving-kindness and compassion as we choose to live like Rebekah and be able to respond to any opportunity God presents to fulfill His plan. It is that same chesed that allows us to follow the Spirit like Mary did as she sat at Christ's feet. And when we revert to our Martha ways, we are able to find great peace in Christ as He patiently takes our hand and leads us on. And we smile, knowingly, at how Martha responded because we can be so much like her! Indeed, it is often easier to be Martha than to be Mary, and yet when we live in the Spirit, making those distinctions becomes less complicated in our everyday lives.

All these women provide us with inspiration to live in accordance to the priorities of God. We also learn the need for intercessory prayer, both on our behalf and ours on the behalf of others. Most importantly, we learn the value of working with God and taking our lead from Him, according to His word. This is evidenced quite clearly in Rebekah's story, specifically in Genesis 24:21 when we are made fully aware of the need to spend time in silence to "hear" God's response to our prayers, being able to accept that the silence may be a minute, an hour, a month or seemingly a lifetime.

These women help us learn to act and react in ways that are pleasing to God and fulfilling to ourselves.

Lord,

Let my heart be fertile ground for Your word.

Let my ears be ever open to Your message.

Let my spirit be always guided by Your love.

Let my countenance be witness to Your abiding love in my life.

In all that I do and in all that I am.

I thank you for always being at my side.

In Christ's name.

Amen

The Word of God

The man watched her the whole time, silently waiting to learn whether or not the Lord had made his errand successful. *Genesis 24:21*

The babies jostled each other within her, and she said, "Why is this happening to me?" So she went to inquire of the Lord. The Lord said to her, "Two nations are in your womb, and two peoples from within you will be separated; one people will be stronger than the other, and the older will serve the younger." *Genesis 25:22-23*

The Lord delights in those who fear him, who put their hope in his unfailing love. *Psalm 147: 13*

All this you were allowed to see that you might know the Lord is God and there is no other. *Deuteronomy 4:35*

Then he prayed, "O Lord, God of my master Abraham, give me success today, and show kindness to my master Abraham. See, I am standing beside this spring, and the daughters of the townspeople are coming out to draw water. May it be that when I say to a girl, 'Please let down your jar that I may have a drink,' and she says, 'Drink, and I'll water your camels too'-let her be the one you have chosen for your servant Isaac. By this I will know that you have shown kindness to my master." *Genesis 24:12-14*

Therefore will I proclaim you, O Lord, among the nations, and I will sing praise to your name. 2 Samuel 22:50

Then he turned toward the woman and said to Simon, "Do you see this woman? I came into your house. You did not give me any water for my feet, but she wet my feet with her tears and wiped them with her hair. You did not give me a kiss, but this woman, from the time I entered, has not stopped kissing my feet. You did not put oil on my head, but she has poured perfume on my feet. Therefore, I tell you, her many sins have been forgiven-for she loved much..." Luke 7:44-47

Have no anxiety at all, but in everything, by prayer and petition, with thanksgiving, make your requests known to God. Then the peace of God that surpasses all understanding will guard your hearts and mind in Christ Jesus. Philippians 4:6-7

Invoking a blessing on Rebekah, they said: "Sister, may you grow into thousands of myriads; And may your descendants gain possession of the gates of their enemies!" Genesis 24:60

Intercession

As Christian women we often find ourselves offering to pray for others. Or we find ourselves asking others for their prayers. This week you will make a concerted effort to pray for those to whom you have promised your prayers as well as for others that you feel guided to pray for. Each day identify one person or family for which you will specifically pray and raise them up to God as you say their name out loud. Follow this with a simple "Glory Be," "Our Father," or any other anointed words you are comfortable using.

Day One-

Today I lift _____
to You, Almighty God.

Day Two-

Today I lift _____
to You, Almighty God.

Day Three-

Today I lift _____
to You, Almighty God.

Day Four-

Today I lift _____
to You, Almighty God.

Day Five-

Today I lift _____
to You, Almighty God.

It is evident that women are meant to form part of the living and working structure of Christianity in so prominent a manner that perhaps not all their potentialities have yet been made clear.

Mulieris Dignitatem

Rachel

Rachel became Rebekah's daughter-in-law when she married Rebekah's favorite son, Jacob. Rachel appears to be, by all accounts, a strong-willed, solid-minded young lady. Her nerve and her conviction are quite admirable and set the tone for her self-confident approach to God.

Like Sarah and Rebekah before her, Rachel is unable to conceive. However, whereas Abraham and Isaac call upon the Lord to open their wives' wombs, Rachel herself implores the Lord for a child. Here we see the wife of Jacob, heir to the Lord's promises, taking matters into her own hands. She needs no intercessor. She is able bodied and confident enough to know what she wants and go about getting it.

Rachel is a woman with many admirable traits. Traits that we know are valued in Scripture. She is strong, resilient, and sure of herself in God. She shows us that even as early as Genesis, the Lord is giving us beautiful examples of women who are capable and bold.

Rachel easily assumes her own right to call upon God to fulfill her most heartfelt desire: to have a child. As such, Rachel's story empowers all women in their right to stand before God and seek their heart's desires. There are often times when we feel burdened by our guilt or unworthy to make request of God. But, through the redemption of Jesus and with a repentant heart, our God welcomes a dialogue with us. So, while we see through Sarah and Rebekah that there are times when intercession is necessary and desirable, we witness through Rachel the times when intercession is unnecessary.

When living lives guided by the Holy Spirit we are more capable of discerning these moments where we can confidently approach God. We learn, through contemplative actions, to listen to the still, small voice that tugs at our heart and guides us. We learn to know when our hopes and dreams are in keeping with God's will in our life. And from that knowledge we acquire the confidence that comes from walking with God.

It is no wonder that we are drawn to Rachel's strength just as Jacob must have been. Nor is it out of character that Jacob's relationship with Rachel also began without intercession. Whereas Abraham sent his servant to find a wife for Isaac, Isaac simply sent Jacob on his way to find a wife. Isaac's only parting remarks to Jacob were, just as Abraham's wishes were for Isaac,

"Do not marry a Canaanite woman. Go at once to Paddan Aram, to the house of your mother's father Bethuel. Take a wife

for yourself there, from among the daughters of Laban, your mother's brother. May God Almighty bless you and make you fruitful and increase your numbers until you become a community of peoples." Genesis 28:1-3

While Jacob was his mother's favorite because of his mild manner (remember that he was a man of the tents - a "homebody," whereas his brother Esau was a hunter) it is easy to see why he would have been so drawn to Rachel. Indeed their meeting was, just like Rebekah and Isaac's, one of love at first sight; at least on the side of Jacob! Meeting her at a well, just as his mother was at a well and accepted the marriage offer made on Isaac's behalf, Rachel, too, exhibited the same qualities of strength, chesed, and compassion. Indeed, she was self-assured and competent as she alone tended the flock in her role as young shepherdess.

As we have often heard, opposites tend to attract and with that, we have an interesting, vibrant Old Testament marriage. We know from scripture that Jacob so loved Rachel that, after having worked seven years as his 'bride price' for her, and then being tricked into marrying her older sister Leah, he quickly committed to another seven years so that he might still marry Rachel. Her countenance was such that Jacob could not walk away from her. Instead, he willingly gave another chunk of his life to her father who was, by all accounts, a deceitful man.

Eventually Rachel and Jacob marry and Rachel's longing for a child fuels a competition with her sister, Leah. It seems especially consoling to see that when the women in the bible display the same characteristics and emotions that we exhibit, like envy or jealousy, our magnificent God still loves them unconditionally. And from that we know that He loves us too, in all our weaknesses and faults.

Hopefully we can also see from this particular heart-wrenching saga of jealous competition that, with God, there is enough anointings, enough blessings for everyone. It would seem that a state of envy is, in fact, a statement of disbelief or distrust in Gods plan for us. Envy essentially translates into a declaration to God that sounds like, "I'm not happy or content with where I am in life or what I have." This is really not an assertion we want to make. Preferably we want to move forward in gratitude and faith, believing that God is working in our lives and His omniscience is to be trusted.

When Rachel finally gives birth it is to the beloved Joseph, the favored son of Jacob. It is Rachel to whom the Gospel of Matthew refers in 2:18. Here Matthew is telling about the birth of Jesus, the way in which the Magi deceived Herod, and the ensuing consequences: all Hebrew boys under two years old were to be killed. Matthew tells us that what the prophet Jeremiah said had been fulfilled.

A voice was heard in Ramah, sobbing and loud lamentation; Rachel weeping for her children, and she would not be consoled, since they were no more.

In this way Rachel is intimately connected to Mary, mother of Jesus, as well. Just as Rachel's soul would mourn the terrible massacre of infant boys in Bethlehem, Mary would mourn the devastating crucifixion of her son. Indeed, her heart would be pierced.

So in Rachel we are presented with a wonderfully strong, capable woman who quite confidently stands before God with her hopes and dreams. But we also see a woman whose soul would experience great pain in the slaughter, generations later, of Hebrew babies. She is, as most of us are, a complex woman. Strong enough to stand before the Lord and make her requests known but fragile in her heart as she weeps for the massacred babies. She exhibits the tremendous strength that so many of us possess and teaches us to pursue our heart's desire when it is surely in keeping with God. Ultimately reminding us that it is, as we have been told, in our heart that the Father seeks us.

Just as we saw Rachel confidently going to the Lord in the Old Testament, we have the bleeding woman approaching the Lord in the New Testament. She boldly pushes through a crowd to touch the edge of Jesus' cloak. Like Rachel before her, this woman intrinsically knows the importance of her own responsibility in her life. She goes after what she wants and believes that she will receive it. This particular woman knows that if she only touches Jesus' robe, she will experience the healing she has sought for a dozen years. She goes right to the source.

This is a perfect understanding of Jesus in our life. He is completely "there" for us. We might get jostled along the way, but when we persevere, we find success. Making the effort to move ourselves forward only speaks of our unwavering faith: a sure pleasure to Jesus.

As a word of caution, in the story of the persistent widow we hear the Lord say, "...*However, when the Son of Man comes, will he find faith on the earth?*" *Luke 18:8.* He is asking us, challenging us, to put our faith under a microscope. He wants us to examine our faith in light of our life's circumstances. Do we maintain our faith when the chips are down? Do we rally around our Creator when it seems as if He is nowhere to be found? These are the times that we show our true faith. This is why Scripture values traits like perseverance and diligence. When we endure through our difficulties, having faith in the Father, then we are professing our unwavering belief in Him.

We should then, like Rachel and the bleeding woman, show faith through our bold confidence in approaching the Lord and trusting in His presence. It is through our experiences, and uncertain or distressing times, that we are able to further develop and enjoy a mutually loving relationship with God. We are not, then, faith-weather friends. We know and savor the bond that exists between Creator and creation because we have participated in its development. Nothing separates us, or keeps us, from God's love and His working in our life. We then confidently stand before the Lord: faithfully loving and trusting Him.

Lord,

I thank you for the courage
to stand before You,
faithfully trusting in Your plan for me.

I am grateful for Your edicts,
knowing that they are a lamp to my feet.

I praise Your holy name
and humbly share my deepest thoughts with You.

I earnestly implore Your will in my life.

My love pours out to You
as my heart cries Your beloved name.

My soul yearns for You.
You are my friend,
my confidant,
and my destiny.

May all the days of my life
give glory to Your sacred name.

In all things I stand before You
through Christ.

Amen

The Word of God

And in his name the Gentiles will hope. Matthew 12:21

Lord my God, in you I take refuge. Psalm 7:2

She said to herself, "If only I can touch his cloak, I shall be cured." Matthew 9:21

Then God remembered Rachel; he listened to her and opened her womb. She became pregnant and gave birth to a son and said, "God has taken away my disgrace." She named him Joseph, and said, "May the Lord add to me another son." Genesis 30:22-24

As Jesus was on his way, the crowds almost crushed him. And a woman who was bleeding for twelve years, but no one could heal her. She came up behind him and touched the edge of his cloak and immediately her bleeding stopped. Luke 8:42-44

The Lord does not look at the things man looks at. Man looks at the outward appearance, but the Lord looks at the heart. 1 Samuel 16:7b

You are my lamp, O Lord! Oh my God, you brighten the darkness about me. 2 Samuel 22:29

Boldly Standing Before God

Continue praying for other people and their needs but add your own as well.

Day One: Today I lift _____
to you, Lord, and I add my request for...

_____

Day Two: Today I lift _____
to you, Lord, and I add my request for...

_____

Day Three: Today I lift
_____
to you, Lord, and I add my request for...

_____

Day Four: Today I lift _____
to you, Lord, and I add my request for...

_____

Day Five: Today I lift _____
to you, Lord, and I add my request for...

_____

From the beginning of Christ's mission, women show to him and to his mystery a special sensitivity which is characteristic of their femininity.

Mulieris Dignitatem

Leah

The Jewish home is filled with wonder and awe as the Sabbath is ushered in. A very significant part of this weekly celebration consists of blessings bestowed upon family members and gratitude given to Adonai. As part of these blessings a mother or father will direct this specific blessing to the daughters of the home: Ye'simech Elohim ke-Sarah, Rivka, Ra-chel ve-Lay'ah. *May God make you like Sarah, Rebecca, Rachel and Leah.*

What characteristics do these matriarchs have in common, and Leah possess in particular, that would merit such high honor? How have these women been woven into the fabric of our lives through their place in Jewish history? These women were all servants of God and as such give us great examples how He loves us in our own journeys.

Leah, most notably, found great favor as she gave birth to each of her sons and then named them according to how she viewed each birth as it reflected her relationship with Hashem (Hebrew for "The Name").

Leah, often thought of in reference to her "tender eyes," was in fact one of the great female figures in Jewish history because of her place in the birth of the Jewish nation. And while we often tend to pity Leah's predicament due to her lifelong yearning for the love of her husband, that pity would be misplaced. Even though she longed for the love of her husband, she was also given great blessings from God. It is for that reason that Jewish homes today bless their daughters *to be like Leah.*

She was, after all, the mother of six of the sons from which the twelve tribes of Israel are formed. She was also the mother of two additional sons of Jacob through her maidservant, Zilpah. Leah is also the mother of Dinah, Jacob's daughter who is raped and whose rape is avenged by her brothers. In many ways her life appears to be a constant source of sadness and struggle and yet we see that ultimately, Leah was both wife of Israel, for we know that Jacob, after his struggle with an angel, becomes known as Israel; and she was mother of Israel as her last son, Judah, brought forth Judaism.

Leah is, then, correctly viewed as a powerful matriarch of the faith. And as our Christian existence makes it ties to the Jewish faith, we are able to, as Christian women, look to Leah as a role model for many things. Christians are grafted into this heritage through their acceptance of Christ as Lord and Savior. Through this grafting, Christian women are able to look upon the Jewish matriarchs for all the ways in which they teach us how to serve God. Leah's life serves as a model for the times we struggle to overcome our earthly woes in order to live for God; to be Christ-like in our words and our actions regardless of our circumstances.

There are many views on Leah's "tender eyes" and yet, as a Christian, it seems most apparent that her tender eyes, caused by years of weeping over a number of different things, might also be what we call "tears of the Spirit." It makes sense that Leah, considered a prophetess, would weep in her knowledge that the Spirit of God was calling upon her to participate in the creation of the Jewish nation and yet she could not reconcile this with the knowledge that her pre-arranged marriage was to be to Esau.

As a woman of great spiritual prowess Leah would have known from an early age that Esau was not cut out to be a patriarch of the faith. In fact, Leah would have understood, on a very deep level, that Jacob had usurped Esau's blessing in an almost righteous way. So her weeping would have been instigated by Rebekah's agreement, early on, with Laban (Rebekah's brother), that Esau and Jacob were intended for Leah and Rachel. Knowing that she was being called to bring forth a Jewish nation, Leah's tears would have been tears of sorrow because her heart would have ached to participate in God's plan as she knew she supposed to do but knowing full well Esau's inability to take on such a role.

This would also explain why Leah agreed to her father's infamously deceitful plan to give her to Jacob when Jacob had expected to be married to Rachel. It seems quite clear that Leah, while never abandoning her hope and desire to be loved by her husband, was willing to put aside her own wishes for happiness in order to fulfill the destiny to which she was called; a destiny fulfilled in her marriage to Jacob. At some point Jacob, too, must have understood that God's call for Leah was to help bring forth a Jewish nation.

The birth of Leah's sons played a pivotal role in her place as matriarch of the faith; as they gave rise to half of the twelve tribes of Israel. Leah's first son, Reuben, was the first born of all Jacob's children. God saw that Leah had boldly gone forth with His call on her life and rewarded her for her interior beauty that was found in her strength and spirit. While He kept Rachel's womb closed, He opened Leah's.

Genesis places much emphasis on Rachel's physical beauty but not on Leah's. Almost to the contrary we read about her weak eyes. But it is in this physical lack that her inner beauty is able to shine. She helps us recognize that God does, in fact, look into our hearts.

Furthermore, the Jewish faith teaches that there are many blessings when one performs a good deed; a mitzvah. God would have looked upon Leah's mitzvah of entering a loveless marriage and granted her the blessing of children. This first born, then, is a recognition of the need and importance of performing good deeds for others and for the glory of His kingdom. With Reuben's birth we also see Leah's continued hope that her husband will come to love her as she chooses the baby's name which, in essence, says, *Because Hashem has seen my humiliation, for my husband will now love me.* Unfortunately, this does not turn out to be the case and yet we will see from Leah's life that she continues to trust in God and live for His call upon her life.

Leah's second son is born and she also gives him a name that reflects her unending belief in God's graces. In many ways she simply refuses to believe that hope does not exist. She says, *Because Hashem has heard that I am not favored, He has given me this one also; and she called his name, Shimon.* Although the birth of this son does not bring Leah into the folds of Jacob's heart, nor satisfy her own longings for love, we see that she continues to trust in God as she becomes pregnant with a third son. With his birth she says, *This time my husband will become attached to me because I have born him three sons; that is why she named him, Levi.* This son, Levi, begins the lineage of the Jewish priesthood; a mighty and powerful statement of how God blesses Leah.

Finally, Leah's forth son is born and named Judah. He is the father of the monarchy of Judaism and also plays an important role in the brothers' experience before Joseph in regards to Benjamin. Judah is also considered, by Leah, to be "more than her fair share of children" and recognizing the tremendous blessing from God for this fourth son she says, *This time I will praise the Lord.* With this birth Leah reveals how to move softly from faith, hope, and trust and into praise. What a beautiful lesson for us!

It is after the birth of Leah's four sons that she gives her maidservant to Jacob and two more sons are born before Leah, again, gives birth to the last three of her children: Issachar, Zeubulun, and Dinah.

Leah, along with Abraham, Isaac, Jacob, Sarah, and Rebekah, is buried in the Cave of Machpelah. She is, interestingly, buried next to Jacob. The Cave of Machpelah is considered to be the second holiest place in the Jewish faith after the Temple Mount in Jerusalem. Rachel is the only matriarch to be buried elsewhere. She is buried near Bethlehem.

We should rightly marvel, then, as Leah moves from complete hope and trust in God to the beautifully simple statement of praise, even though her earthly desire to be in a loving relationship with Jacob does not seem to manifest. Let us recognize that she captures for us the need to have complete trust and faith in God for our needs and desires. But, more importantly, she teaches us how to turn our hope, faith, and trust into simple praise when all is said and done.

Lord,

May I please You as Leah had done
in a selfless and loving way.

May my action always reflect my understanding
that You are the source of all this is,
was and ever shall be.

Please guide me as I do my best to put aside my own
interests and desires and to join You,
more fully, in my daily living.

I thank you for Your graces and
mercy that have allowed me
to be grafted into Your kingdom.

Through Christ, I praise, worship, and glorify You.

Amen

The Word of God

He has made everything beautiful in its time. He has also set eternity in the hearts of men; yet they cannot fathom what God has done from beginning to end. I know that there is nothing better for men than to be happy and do good while they live. That everyone may eat and drink, and find satisfaction in all his toil-this is the gift of God. Ecclesiastes 3:11-13

Come to me, all you who are weary and burdened, and I will give you rest. Take my yoke upon you and learn from me, for I am gentle and humble in hearts, and you will find rest for your souls. For my yoke is easy and my burden is light. Matthew 11:28-30

Finish this daughter's bridal week; then we will give you the younger one also, in return for another seven years of work. And Jacob did so. Genesis 29:27-28

Dear friends, if our hearts do not condemn us, we have confidence before God and receive from him anything we ask, because we obey his commands and do what pleases him. 1 John 3:21-22

However, if you suffer as a Christian, do not be ashamed, but praise God that you bear that name. 1 Peter 4:1

Trusting in God

Even though Leah did not see the love from her husband that she longed for, her trust and faith in God never ebbed. She continued to praise and trust in Him through her whole life and thus became a matriarch of the faith. Leah shows us how to praise God even in the absence of what our heart desires.

Consider ways in which your trust in God ebbs and flows. Write a journal entry about this and ask for His hand in helping you overcome any obstacles that are in your way to a fully committed relationship with Him in which you are able to give praise even in the absence of what your heart longs for.

_____
_____
_____
_____
_____
_____
_____
_____
_____
_____
_____

Motherhood is the fruit of the marriage union of a man and woman, of that biblical "knowledge" which corresponds to the "union of the two in one flesh."

Mulieris Dignitatem

Shiphrah and Puah

Before Pharaoh's daughter scoops Moses out of the Nile, Scripture introduces us to two Hebrew midwives. These women, Shiphrah and Puah, put their lives on the line in disobeying a directive from Pharaoh while ultimately being in obedience to God. They disregard Pharaoh's orders to kill all newborn Hebrew baby boys and in so doing teach us two wonderful aspects important to our roles as women of faith.

First, and foremost, these women teach us how to make our choices, regardless of consequences, based on the right fear of God. Recall that 'fear of the Lord' is a gift of the Holy Spirit. They teach us that fear of God is, in actuality, a fear of displeasing God. Fear of God is a right-placed knowledge that, in displeasing God, we jeopardize our relationship with Him. The fear comes from the realization of what our lives would be like without God.

Second, Shiphrah and Puah are examples of following the natural law that God placed in our heart. A law that connects us to God and exists in each and every one of us: a way that our conscience guides us and our spirit stays united to God. In disobeying Pharaoh's clear instructions, but following the natural law written in their hearts, these women live out the first and the sixth commandments, **prior** to Moses receiving them in written form.

The First Commandment, *"You shall have no other gods before Me."* quite succinctly prioritizes our very existence. When it comes to rulers, authority, and the levels of any hierarchy, God trumps all. The idea that Shiphrah and Puah understand this before it exists in written form emphasizes the fact that there is a natural law, written upon our hearts, that draws us to God in all our circumstances. And, being guided by the Spirit, we are able to respond to that law, knowingly and without trepidation. Shiphrah and Puah give us a beautiful example of the natural law that forever tugs at us, pulling us towards God.

The Sixth Commandment, *"You shall not murder."* also resides soundly in their hearts. We can look to Shiphrah and Puah as the first women to boldly live a pro-life message. And in living this message, which is pleasing to God, we find that they received blessings of their own. They made a difficult decision in the face of disobeying Pharaoh and yet stayed committed to their God, our God. When Pharaoh's edict came in conflict with their God's edict, as revealed to them in their hearts, they chose God.

More and more our secular lives are encroaching upon our Christian values and, like Shiphrah and Puah, we are in positions where we must take a stand. We should look to these women as heroines whose fear of displeasing God was the determining factor in the decisions they made.

Shiphrah and Puah faced two realities when they received the directive from Pharaoh to kill newborn Hebrew baby boys. They understood that one was a temporary reality while the other was an eternal reality. The first reality was to understand what would happen in disobeying Pharaoh. With this reality was the potential for severe or even life-or-death consequences. However, these wise women also understood that these consequences, regardless of their severity, were transitory. Let us recall, by meditating upon their actions, that wisdom is a gift of the Spirit and proceeds from fear of the Lord.

The second reality these women understood was the necessity of obeying God. Shiphrah and Puah were not willing to disobey the God they served. For them, the everlasting consequences of this must have far outweighed the temporal consequences of disobeying Pharaoh. So, in a few short verses we see two women using their free will in a noble and profound way. We see two women taking the first pro-life stand in the book of Exodus.

Undoubtedly current secularism makes us face our pro-life commitments in uncomfortable and often unpopular ways. However, like Shiphrah and Puah, we too must take a stand. We, too, must witness to the value of each human life. We must also respond to the natural law written in our hearts in which God reminds us that He determines the beginning and end of each of our lives. We are called to work with Him in all aspects of life knowing that He will, one day, welcome us home with open arms. And on that day we will give an accounting of our life on earth. We want that accounting to be pleasing to Him and without regrets.

After we learn that Shiphrah and Puah disobey Pharaoh to obey God, their brief story ends in the simplest of lines. We read...*And because the midwives feared God, he gave them families of their own.* No fanfare, just a fundamental recognition of the favor we find with God when we choose to do His work. Often the favor includes earthly benefits but always the favor includes heavenly blessings.

Let us be inspired by Shiphrah and Puah's example of pro-life decisions, in obedience to the awesome God that we serve, knowing that our rewards come in eternal packages. Women today are able to speak in a multitude of ways. They speak through the values they impart to their children and how they spend their time. They speak through the dollars they spend and the shows they watch. Women speak through their vote and through the alliances they maintain. Shiphrah and Puah, whose mention is so fleeting in Exodus, remind us that our lives, too, are just as fleeting and the stands we take are just as important. They show us that all the legislation written, passed, and amended will not replace the natural law that God lovingly placed within our hearts.

Lord,

My heart rests with You
And the knowledge of Your ways.

My heart aches to please You
And to abide in Your presence.

My heart is filled
With a longing that only You can fill.

Let me always remember
That the things of this earth are passing

But Your love never ends.

Amen

The Word of God

I urge you, brothers, to watch out for those who cause divisions and put obstacles in your way that are contrary to the teaching you have learned. Keep away from them. Romans 16:17

You shall not murder. Genesis 20:13

The mind of a sinful man is death, but the mind controlled by the Spirit is life and peace. Romans 8:6

The king of Egypt said to the Hebrew midwives, whose names were Shiphrah and Puah, "When you help the Hebrew women in childbirth and observe them on the delivery stool, if it is a boy, kill him; but if it is a girl, let her live," The midwives, however feared God and did not do what the king of Egypt had told them to do; they let the boys live...So God was kind to the midwives and the people increased and became even more numerous. And because the midwives feared God, he gave them families of their own. Exodus 1:15-21

Those controlled by the sinful nature cannot please God. You, however, are controlled not by the sinful nature but by the Spirit, if the Spirit of God lives in you. Romans 8:8-9

Living God's Word

Look for ways this week to show your commitment to learning and living according to God's Word. Shiphrah and Puah were the first "Pro-Life" advocates. Consider the ways in which you can honor God's word through your actions. By the end of the week be able to record at least one instance in which your conduct spoke louder than any words could have.

This week I made a difference. I honored the Word of God when I...

_____
_____
_____
_____
_____
_____
_____
_____
_____
_____
_____
_____

Created in the image and likeness of God as a "unity of the two," both have been called to a spousal love.

Mulieris Dignitatem

Zipporah

Like so many other women in our world, we know about Zipporah through the success of her husband. Of course, not many of our husbands have such name recognition as Moses, but the story is the same. Oftentimes we find ourselves in the background, nurturing our friends, our spouses, our children, and our neighbors. And, like Zipporah, we have a name and a commitment to the ones we love but it isn't necessarily our name that the world or the community might know. Or our role is diminished because it is the less sought after role of homemaker or mother. Fortunately for us, the Lord will know the fruits of our love. He will recognize our dedication to those in He put in our lives and in our corner of the world.

Scripture gives us role models for nurturers as well as for prophetesses and judges. We see women summoned by God in numerous ways. And regardless of the summons, God's hand is evident in the uniqueness of each and every call. Of course the secular messages aren't always as evident. We often struggle to find our place, as defined by the world. However, when we are guided by the Holy Spirit we are able to cut through the cloudiness of the secular messages that are, at once, loud and yet contradictory.

We have all, in one way or another, experienced the haziness of the world's messages. We might even have found it difficult to be at peace with what feels "right" because we are often told that it is "wrong." If we are at home, raising children, the world tells us that we will miss opportunities in our careers. If we choose our careers society tells us that we will miss our child's first steps and first words. If we remain childless the world tells us that we are selfish. If we have six children we are treated as if we are irresponsible. The tumultuousness of the messages takes its toll.

When we find ourselves in the midst of this, it is crucial to bring our focus back to God. When we surrender our lives to Him, He can work with us as He sees fit: not as the world tells us, nor as our false sense of "truth" tells us.

Zipporah, then, is the great reminder that God's plans are often in absolute contrast to what we might have planned or what we might be told is "right." And she then shows us how to gracefully accept what the Lord puts on our plate. Most certainly her life unfolded in a way that was in stark contrast to what she would have imagined. We ought to find great faith in that simple realization. From it we can clearly see that the Lord always knows what is best for each and everyone of us and willingly looks to work with us to that end.

It would seem safe to say that while Zipporah was tending to sheep and found the stranger, Moses, at the well, she did not conceive of what lay ahead. Could she have fathomed, even for an instant, that this man would soon be her husband and in direct communication with God - talking to a burning bush and receiving commandments? If she imagined herself as a wife and mother it would, no doubt, have been in very conventional ways. But her resolve to love and support her husband allowed God's plan to unfold. And, as it turned out, it was a very unconventional, complex plan which included parting a huge body of water and multiple plagues! So when Zipporah participated in God's plans, she was able to be all that God hoped for and needed her to be.

In a very trusting and loving way, Zipporah went along with the life that was developing. She shows us that her part in Exodus was as valuable to God's plans as was Moses receiving the Ten Commandments and parting the Red Sea. After all, had she wanted to make things difficult for Moses, we all know she could have. She could have, like Eve, forever changed the course of human history.

Instead she relied on her confidence as a wife, mother, and woman. She was not affected by the realization that her life, her marriage, was anything other than what she had probably dreamt about. In Moses' life Zipporah was the perfect compliment to his mother. Herself a woman whose faith in God allowed her to release Moses into the Nile. When we meditate on the women in Moses' life, it is no wonder that he was able to build the most loving of relationships with God. He was himself blessed with women in his life who were resolute in their faith. These women were able to turn everything over to God, fully trusting in His omniscience.

Zipporah's everyday life shows us that she was strong, loving, and faithful. She was both self-confident and self-effacing at the same time. She had to be all these things, and more, to live a life outside of the normal expectations as her husband moved forward in God's plan for the Hebrew people. She was a mighty and powerful woman. Consider, even for a brief moment, how accomplishing her role also allowed Moses to reach his destiny for God and ultimately scribe the Torah. It is both illuminating and exhilarating for those of us in positions to offer nurturing and support to others. Indeed, it inspires us to embrace the opportunities that the Holy Spirit gives us in which we can help one another in our walk with God.

Indeed, we should all recognize that we have the same influencing power that Zipporah possessed. So if our life is one of nurturing and support, and it is dismissed, we should recall how Zipporah's nurturing love allowed Moses to free God's people. Whatever she did on the "home-front" allowed Moses to wholeheartedly tend to God's people. It was in that supportive way that she had an enormous effect on a multitude of people.

We see from Zipporah that a woman who loves and encourages her spouse, her children, or her friends is actually able to impact a tremendous amount of people. It literally becomes her character that moves out into the world through these people. Her kindness and her compassion are able to take on a life of their own. A woman's influence, and her subsequent responsibility, should never be underestimated.

And, of course, the opposite is true. A difficult, angry, unkind woman just as easily sends negative or detrimental energy out into the world. As we recall from Sarah, our behavior always has an affect on others. At the end of our lives we will come face to face with God. We will be held responsible for our words and our actions. It will be at that point that the realization of how we treated others will most fully impact us. We will learn how we have affected others' lives. We will be held accountable. We would do well, then, to learn from Zipporah the intrinsic value of creating a loving, supportive home.

Make no mistake about it; women are very powerful creatures. How we use that power is of our own choosing.

Do we, like Zipporah, allow God's plan to unfold, especially if it is different than we had imagined? Do we trust God and the path that He has put us on? Or do we hinder Him in untold ways? Are we brave enough, like Zipporah, to find our worth in a solid marriage or do we let others shake our foundation?

Consider King David's wife Abigail, a woman very much like Zipporah, powerfully imbued with the Spirit of God. As David's third wife, she was the one who brought to David a harmony he had not yet experienced. Abigail intercepted David as he was on his way to kill her first husband, himself apparently a greedy, stupid man who refused to reciprocate David's guardianship over land and animals. Right away we see that Abigail is able to grasp the seriousness of the situation that alluded her husband and in that way spared his life from David's impending plan. This is exceedingly similar to Zipporah saving Moses' life when God was out to kill him (see Genesis 4:24-26). We read that Zipporah, imbued with the Spirit, understood the ways of God and stepped in to keep Moses from harm.

Just so, Abigail knew immediately upon approaching David that she was in the presence of greatness from God and bowed to show her respect and understanding. While David went on to have many more wives, it is Abigail who brought the balance into David's life that most assuredly allowed him to continue with his own predestination.

Zipporah's beautiful story, as well as the story of Abigail, is one of trust and courage for married women. Both women reflect that in the Spirit a woman is powerful and resilient. Both encourage us to face the secular skepticism that says we cannot be fully happy or complete in a mutually respectful relationship. Both women show us how to trust our mates and how to trust God.

Zipporah, then, gives us the courage to stand firm when the world tells us to fold. She is a woman whose powerful ability to offer nurturing love and support to a man on a treacherous mission ultimately allowed God's plan for His people to be realized. Abigail, too, reflects what a woman is able to bring to a man and to a home: harmony, nurturance, and stability. These are things to value and uphold. They are things of God and are God-honoring.

God would have known, as His word indicates in Genesis 2:24, that in choosing Moses, He was also choosing Zipporah. She was a woman, like Noah's wife, up to the great task ahead. Like Abigail, Zipporah is truly a woman for all times as she embodies strength, fortitude, and trust. Zipporah, Abigail, Noah's wife; All strong women whose lives illustrate a woman's ability to affect the world from within the walls of her home, from her daily living in the Spirit of God.

Lord,

Thank you for the strength You give me
to live a life pleasing to You.

Let me always remember to have a grateful heart
in whatever circumstances I find myself.

I give You my life, my hopes, and my dreams
confidently knowing that Your plans for me
are far better than any I could ever imagine.

In all ways I trust in You
and eagerly anticipate
all You have in store for me.
Your humble servant,

Amen

The Word of God

For this reason a man will leave his father and mother and be united to his wife, and they will become one flesh. Genesis 2:24

Husbands, love your wives, just as Christ loved the church...In this same way, husbands ought to love their wives as their own bodies. He who loves his wife loves himself...However each of you also must love his wife as he loves himself, and the wife must respect her husband. Ephesians 5:25-33

When one finds a worthy wife her value is far beyond pearls. Proverbs 31:10

And where is he? He asked his daughters, "Why did you leave him? Invite him to have something to eat." Moses agreed to stay with the man, who gave his daughter Zipporah to Moses in marriage. Zipporah gave birth to a son, and Moses named him Gershom, saying, "I have become an alien in a foreign land." Exodus 2:20-22

Then he said, "May the Lord not be angry, but let me speak just once more. What if only ten can be found there?" He answered, "For the sake of ten, I will not destroy it [the city of Sodom]." When the Lord had finished speaking with Abraham, he left and Abraham returned home. Genesis 18:32-33

On the journey, at a place where they spent the night, the Lord came upon Moses and would have killed him. But Zipporah took a piece of flint and cut off her son's foreskin and, touching his person, she said, "You are a spouse of blood to me." Then God let Moses go. Exodus 4:24-25

She [the ideal wife] is clothed with strength and dignity, and she laughs at the days to come. She opens her mouth in wisdom, and on her tongue is kindly counsel. Proverbs 31:25-26

David said to Abigail: "Blessed be the Lord, the God of Israel, who sent you to meet me today. Blessed be your good judgment and blessed be you yourself, who this day have prevented me from shedding blood and from avenging myself personally...1 Samuel 25:32-33

The Sanctity of Marriage

Write your own personal prayer for the marriages of your family, friends, and yourself (if applicable). If you or a particular friend is unmarried, consider writing a prayer that, if the Lord's will is for a marriage, it will be centered on Christ. Find Scripture passages that you can incorporate into your 'Marriage Prayer.' As God knows us by name, make sure you use names in your prayer.

In the Spirit of Christ, in fact, women can discover the entire meaning of their femininity and thus be disposed to making a "sincere gift of self" to others, thereby finding themselves.

Mulieris Dignitatem

Miriam

Miriam's life, as older sister of Moses, is quite mesmerizing. As a young seven-year-old girl, she places her infant brother into a basket and then places that basket into the Nile where, hiding in the reeds, she watches as he is found by Pharaoh's daughter. From there this incredibly brave little girl offers Pharaoh's daughter a nursemaid for this newly found infant; the nursemaid, of course, being Moses' mother. With the great plans that God has in store for Moses, we should not be amazed at the women to whom he was given care: women whose presence in his life, at critical junctures, created an environment for him to answer God; women whose very presence safeguarded his life when it might have otherwise been lost.

He was born of a humble servant, a Hebrew woman whose faith in God allowed her to place her newborn son in a basket to be floated down the Nile. He was given a sister whose bravery belied her young age and who rose to be a significant force in the freeing of the Hebrew slaves. Finally, Moses marries an Ethiopian woman, Zipporah, whose acceptance of her husband's call allows Moses to fulfill God's plan most successfully.

Miriam grows from a young child who played a critical role in the survival of Moses to a young woman, defined as Moses as the first prophetess of the Hebrew people. Hundreds of years after her death, the prophet Micah reminded the Hebrews that three people freed them from slavery: Moses, Aaron, and Miriam. This is quite a significant recognition given to her. We also know that, during this event in which Micah gives her equal credit for releasing the Israelites from Egyptian slavery, Miriam was a formidable presence whose song of praise to God greatly inspired the Hebrew women. In all aspects of her life she moved with God, just as her younger brother did.

Maybe that is why, when she and Aaron let the fruits of their spirit become mired in envy, God chose a swift punishment for her: leprosy. Prior to the exchange in which Miriam and Aaron questioned Moses being the only recipient of God's words, Miriam consistently produced the fruits that Christ said we will be known by: love, joy, peace, longsuffering, gentleness, goodness, faith, meekness and temperance.

Until that time, Miriam had lovingly and joyfully served God, who reciprocally elevated her to the same status as Aaron. Her countenance was one of peace and longsuffering for her people. Her goodness was evident in her life as a young child following her mother's wishes and safeguarding her brother. So when she let her envy cloud her judgment and fell prey to "bad-mouthing" God's most humble servant, Moses, God's punishment was speedy and without regard to her status. In that, we see that our own journey's are always under the scrutiny of the laws set down by Christ. Does our salvation depend upon our unerring following of these edicts? No. Nevertheless, we are called to produce the fruits of the Spirit in ways that our lives reflect Christ's workings within us.

As we would imagine, Moses does plead to God for Miriam's healing and it is given. However, as we serve a righteous God, we see that Miriam must still suffer consequences for her actions and she is dispelled from her community for seven days. The message: God is a just God, even to those who most faithfully serve Him. Does He not withhold Moses from entering the Promised Land? He does. And we know that no one was ever more loved than Moses to whom God admittedly spoke face-to-face.

Should this fact frighten us or deter us from our lifelong quest of perseverance for the race set before us? It should not. From the tender age of seven, we see that Miriam's life was truly a "lifelong" journey.

We learn from Miriam that even on our most graced days, we are often tempted to be less than Christian. Even when we are surrounded by God's mercy and blessings, we must rise above the secular circumstances in which we live. While some of our battles will be easily won, others will require intercession. We may rely on our friends and family for aid in an earthly manner or for spiritual help in the way of prayers. And the opposite is true as well. We are called to help others in their journey's: whether through intercessory prayer or with earthly support in difficult and trying circumstances. Miriam's life is also a reflection on the joy and inspiration we can supply to others. As Christians we rely heavily upon community; both as participants and as recipients. God has always called us to be in community, knowing that we each possess different gifts that glorify His kingdom; all necessary and equally important.

Ultimately, Miriam's life emphasizes how God calls each of us to work within our own circumstances for His kingdom and to recognize our total and complete reliance on Him as sovereign Lord and Creator. With Him we are able to do everything. Without Him we are as helpless as newborn babes.

Lord,

Sovereign Creator and Righteous Father:

May we,
like Miriam,
know your blessings and graces
all the days of our lives.

May we see in Miriam
how Your hand guides all things.

May we be those instruments
that bring You glory and praise
while recognizing our complete reliance on You.

May the fruits our Your Spirit
be evident in all we say and do as we call upon you,
"Abba! Abba!"

Do not turn Your ear from us
but in Your mercy and kindness.
heed our words
delivered with humble and contrite hearts.

We ask all things through Your most beloved Son.
Jesus. The Christ.

Amen

The Word of God

He who guards his mouth protects his life; to open wide one's lips brings downfall. Proverbs 13:3

For I brought you up from the land of Egypt, from the place of slavery I released you; And I sent you Moses, Aaron, and Miriam. Micah 6:4

His sister stationed herself at a distance to find out what would happen to him. Exodus 2:4

Then his sister asked Pharaoh's daughter, "Shall I go and call one of the Hebrew women to nurse the child for you?" Exodus 3:7

The prophetess Miriam, Aaron's sister, took a tambourine in her hands, while all the women went out after her with tambourines, dancing; and she led them in the refrain: Sing to the Lord, for he is gloriously triumphant; horse and chariot he has cast into the sea. Exodus 15:20-21

Finally, brothers, rejoice. Mend your ways, encourage one another, agree with one another, live in peace, and the God of love and peace will be with you. 2 Corinthians 13:11

Encourage One Another

While we learn from Miriam that it is our call to watch and guard our tongue, we also learn how we are called to encourage and inspire one another as she so often did.

This week look for an opportunity to live both these lessons from Miriam. First, be on the watch for a time where your words are better left unsaid. Second, be on the watch for a time where your words can be of the encouraging, inspiring kind that will reveal Christ's light and love to the world. Record your experiences.

_____
_____
_____
_____
_____
_____
_____
_____
_____
_____
_____
_____
_____
_____
_____
_____

The Church gives thanks for all the manifestations of the feminine "genius" which have appeared in the course of history, in the midst of all peoples and nations; she gives thanks for all the charisms which the Holy Spirit distributes to women in the history of the People of God, for all the victories which she owes to their faith, hope and charity; she gives thanks for all the fruits of feminine holiness.

Mulieris Dignitatem

Deborah

Understanding the story of Deborah, a prophetess and judge, begins with a general understanding of the history of God's people, the Israelites. Deborah, like many of the women in our faith history, was herself Jewish. She ruled over God's people with fairness and insight.

From the time of Genesis, in which God created Adam and Eve, to the time of Deborah, the people of God had been in and out of His favor numerous times. During these tumultuous times they both angered Him as well as cried out to Him for deliverance. From chapter three in Judges to chapter four in Judges we hear three different instances when the Israelites offended God, fell under the power of a foreign ruler, and then cried out to God for help and forgiveness. It has been said that, as a result of each of these upheavals, the Hebrew people drew closer to God.

Nonetheless, at the time of Deborah we find that the Israelites had again offended God and were being oppressed by a Canaanite king whose army was under the rule of General Sisera. Judges had been governing the Israelites who, unlike any neighboring nations, recognized the one true God. These judges, like Deborah, had the respect due their position. People would take their troubles and disagreements to the judge. The judge would administer rulings, admonishments, and consequences. For the Israelite people, God was king but there was still a need for earthly jurisprudence. That was the role and responsibility of the judges: to maintain civility and equity among the people. For many years this was the way in which the Hebrew people conducted their daily affairs.

Deborah's beautiful story shows us how God will call women to all positions and walks in life. He determines who is best suited in a particular set of circumstances. It is then our responsibility to fill our role with the Scripture characteristics that are held in high esteem: perseverance, joy, gratitude, and wisdom among others. Deborah, herself, would have been a role model for characteristics that the Lord values.

She would have embodied the traits necessary to be a judge for the Jewish people. In that role, the traits would have particularly included strength, wisdom, and wealth. But we would not understand the meaning of these traits by applying today's definitions. Just like we often misunderstand the meaning of humility when serving the Lord, we would probably misunderstand the meanings implied by these adjectives as well.

For instance, Deborah's strength would have been reflected in her ability to conquer her natural desires. As we learn from Eve, succumbing to temptation is much easier than walking away from it. And yet, this is what we must train ourselves to do. So Deborah would have displayed an ability to overcome the desires of the flesh and to walk more fully in the Spirit. As we know, this doesn't happen without a deep and trusting relationship with God. We can assume that her relationship with the Father would have given her the strength needed in her earthly walk to overcome the temptations in her life.

There is a saying that a smart man learns from his own mistakes and a wise man learns from others'. This is how Deborah would have shown her wisdom. She would have learned from others' mistakes and applied those understandings to situations in her community. As a judge she would have been able to administer justice based upon the experiences of those around her. She would have been able to take lessons learned from one set of circumstances and apply them to other circumstances. And, in so doing, she showed the true meaning of wisdom. Scripture is replete with our call to gain wisdom and Deborah would have been considered "wise" to be called to such a position in her life.

The third characteristic that Deborah would have embodied was wealth. But her wealth would have been evident in her satisfaction with life and an accompanying inner peace. We can assume that instead of complaining about a long "work" day or the petty grievances that she had to hear, she must have begun and ended each day with a gratitude for what it would hold or held. Our world is filled with sagas of greed and treachery. We know from these stories that material wealth does not satisfy the soul. This is why wealth, by Old Testament standards, refers to an inner peace. It is that same inner peace that Jesus left to us. He knew that inner peace was true wealth. And in that way, Deborah was deemed quite wealthy.

Deborah, then, embodies characteristics that God would like us to manifest as well. She was wealthy because of her gratitude for the life that the Lord gave her. She was wise as she continuously applied newly acquired knowledge to a variety of situations. And she was strong in her ability to be guided by the Spirit and to resist the temptations of life. Deborah helps us understand how we can better serve God when we embrace and develop these anointed traits in our own lives. She was qualified to be both a prophetess and judge for the Jewish people. And in that role she was able to bring God's people out from oppression.

As a prophetess and judge Deborah is able to deliver the news of how God's people will be delivered from the tyrannical Canaanite king. Deborah shares this plan with the commander of the Israelite army. In sharing God's plan with the commander, we immediately witness the commander's great dependence on her. He says, *"If you come with me, I will go; if you do not come with me, I will not go."* It seems odd to hear a mighty general saying such things to a woman. Odder yet is her response. In it we recognize her great dependence and trust in God. Recall that, as a prophetess, she was simply revealing God's plan to the general. As such she easily knew her trust in God was well placed and was able to reply saying, *"I will certainly go with you."* She then adds that, although they will have success, the Canaanite general will fall not to the Israelite commander but to a woman. Again a simple sharing of God's plan with no self-aggrandizing attached: strong in following the Spirit, wise in learning from those around her, and wealthy in accepting this role.

In this decisive exchange we see the courage that women must often have in fulfilling their purpose. We also see the extent to which others, even those in great and powerful positions, rely on women. Deborah epitomizes the strength and courage women possess in all walks of life. She shows us that when we are in compliance with God's will, we help make the impossible become possible. Deborah, then, will go with the Israelite commander and conquer the Canaanite army but the Canaanite general, Sisera, will not be conquered in this battle. He will fall to a woman.

True to His word, as delivered through Deborah, God brought the entire Canaanite army down. General Sisera, as expected, escaped. He fled to the tent of Jael, the wife of an ally. Again, as Deborah had prophesized, Sisera fell to a woman: to Jael. With Sisera asleep in her tent, Jael murdered him. With the death of the Canaanite general, and the subsequent humiliation to the Canaanite king, came freedom to the Israelites. From this point we learn that the land had peace for forty years.

There are so many aspects of Deborah's personality that speaks to women of today. She was a respected leader, prophetess, and judge. She showed great trust in the plan that God shared with her and tremendous courage in a very difficult time. She had great generals acquiesce to her authority and was both open and honest in her conduct. Deborah is a beautiful heroine. Her self-assurance is worthy of respect and admiration. Although it would be foolish to imagine that she was without her qualms, she shows us that her confidence and trust in God makes all things possible. And, reciprocally, God was able to work with Deborah because of her humility, faith, and obedience.

Like Deborah, we too, are able to listen to God in our lives. We are right to assume that He would like to guide us, through His spirit, in ways that we might never imagine.

We know that He works all things for His good and we would do well to move forward with the understanding that our role in His plan is both vital and necessary. Just as Deborah accomplished great things for God, we too can accomplish great things for God.

We also have to be fascinated by the role that Jael plays in the fall of the Canaanite general. Here is a woman whose mention, although minor, plays a major role in the history of God's people. Recall that Deborah told the Israelite commander that Sisera, the Canaanite general, would fall to a woman. What a potent statement: the fact that the Israelite army would defeat the entire Canaanite army and yet the Canaanite general, the top man, would fall to a woman. And in Sisera's demise was the ultimate demise of the Canaanites, brought about by a woman following God's call on her life.

When we are given the opportunity to show our might and strength in God, do we heed His call? As disciples of Christ, we are all called for a unique and worthy purpose. We are all placed within a particular set of circumstances, interacting with a given group of friends and acquaintances. Our unique paths allow us to proclaim our faith in both words and deeds. We are, on the one hand, living in a time where worshiping God is neither accepted nor embraced. On the other hand we are also seeing a spread of Christianity to the ends of the earth. It is an interesting dilemma. We can certainly rest assured that we have a role to play that will help God's plan for humanity to unfold. And so, like Deborah, God calls each of us to be strong and faithful to Him.

Trusting in His providence, learning His word, and inviting His active participation in our lives makes our relationship with God vibrant and strong. It is in that symbiotic relationship that we can be called to do His will. He guides, we move, we talk, He listens. Over time the exchanges between our creator and ourselves becomes quite fluid. A synchronicity begins to develop that is both pleasing to God and fulfilling to us. We are walking with Him and begin to fully understand such terms as "fear of the Lord." In connecting with Him our fear is to face a time when we would be without Him. And so, we begin to care more about our relationship with Him than ever before. Like Deborah and Jael before us, we recognize our complete dependence on Him.

Deborah's life, then, is testimony to the great call God has in store for us and our friends and family. Each and every one of us has that unique part to fill: that reason we exist. All pieces, regardless of the worldly view, are critical to God's plan. So, whether we are warriors or judges, whether we are mothers or advocates, our destiny is our own. And God looks for us to fill it with vigor and joy.

Lord,

Thank you for this day You have given me.

In it,
let me rejoice in Your goodness,
let me trust in Your providence.

Like Deborah,
let me embrace Your call upon my life.

Like Deborah,
let my words resound in the trust I have in You.

Like Deborah,
may I always hear and understand Your will,
follow Your guidance, find my strength in You
and be forever at Your service.

Amen

The Word of God

In the same way, the Spirit helps us in our weakness. We do not know what we ought to pray for, but the Spirit himself intercedes for us with groans that words cannot express. And he who searches our hearts knows the mind of the Spirit, because the Spirit intercedes for the saints in accordance with God's will. Romans 8:26-27

Deborah, a prophetess, the wife of Lappidoth, was leading Israel at that time. She held court under the Palm of Deborah between Ramah and Bethel in the hill country of Ephraim, and the Israelites came to her to have their disputes decided. Judges 4:4-5

Sisera, however, fled on foot to the tent of Jael, the wife of Heber the Kenite, because there were friendly relations between Jabin, king of Hazor and the clan of Heber the Kenite. Judges 4:17

For this we toil and struggle, because we have set our hope on the living God, who is the savior of all, especially of those who believe. 1 Timothy 4:10

It was not through law that Abraham and his offspring received the promise that he would be heir of the world, but through the righteousness that comes by faith. Romans 4:13

Sing to the Lord a New Song

Deborah celebrates the Israelite victory with the Canticle of Deborah (*Judges 5*). *On that day Deborah [and Barak, son of Abinoam] sang this song.*

Take the time in the next few days to find at least three different songs that celebrate Jesus' victory over death, your salvation, and the Glory of God. Learn these songs and sing them throughout the days this week. Consider purchasing a CD that contains songs, attending a church service with an eye for the liturgical music, or simply finding a Christian station on your stereo. Whatever way you choose to do it, make an effort to sing your praises to the Lord this week.

The songs I discovered (or rediscovered) this week were:

1. _____

2. _____

3. _____

Every vocation has a profoundly personal and prophetic meaning.

Mulieris Dignitatem

Ruth

Ruth is a Moabite who came to be a daughter-in-law of Naomi, a Hebrew woman. Naomi and her husband, along with their two sons, were forced to leave their town of Bethlehem due to a famine. They traveled to Moab where Elimelech, Naomi's husband, soon died. In Moab, Ruth's sons married Moabite women. One son married Orpah and the other married Ruth. After a decade or so, Naomi's sons also died, leaving Naomi without a husband or children but with two daughters-in-law.

Hearing that the Lord had provided food for the people of Bethlehem, Naomi decided to move back to her home in Bethlehem. She encouraged her daughters-in-law to move on with their lives. Naomi fully expected Orpah and Ruth to stay in Moab and remarry. She must have been a bit taken aback when she heard Ruth's response.

While Orpah agrees to go her own way and sadly says her "good-byes" to Naomi, Ruth refuses to part. She makes the bold claim that nothing but death will separate her from Naomi and Naomi's God. At this point Naomi sees that it would be futile to try to persuade Ruth to stay behind. This must touch Naomi's heart in a way that we can only imagine. Although Naomi had lost her husband and her two sons, she was given the love of family in Ruth.

When we consider that Ruth cannot fathom leaving Naomi, we have to be in awe of what a loving woman Naomi must have been. Certainly we can assume that Naomi was a powerful witness to the Lord and that Ruth's heart was fertile ground for such a message. We are once again reminded how our actions are always affecting others. We are forced to ask ourselves some very powerful questions.

For instance, are we living in such a way that our life is a testimony to our faith? If God puts someone in our life whose heart is fertile ground for the Word, are we sowing potential seeds? The relationship between Naomi and Ruth prompts us to ask tough questions of ourselves, remembering that witnessing to those who share our faith is easy but being able to witness to those outside of our faith is another story. Are we sowing, through words and deeds, in the places that God wants?

As we continue to read the story of Ruth we hear Naomi soon refer to Ruth as her "daughter." She becomes an "adopted" child. Ruth is enfolded into Naomi's life in such a way that the foreshadowing of Gentiles being enfolded into the message of Jesus is quite evident. Ruth, an "outsider," represents the Gentiles who were originally "outsiders" to the Good News. Remember that Ruth is purposely, and with her free will, choosing Naomi's God to call her own. Just as we purposely, and with free will, accept Jesus.

Indeed, Ruth's story is filled with the foreshadowing of our own salvation: her story is one of commitment, redemption, and the lineage of Jesus Christ. Through Ruth we understand what the Lord requires of us to be in His favor: a deep abiding love and free acceptance. Ruth, in both her words and her actions, is a clear and concise example of commitment and love. Her love for Naomi, and subsequently Naomi's God, is what motivates her to leave her old life behind and stay with Naomi. It reminds us that we are all called to witness to the potential "Ruths" in our lives.

We are all called to be beacons of light to others. So, just as Naomi's countenance was able to draw Ruth to the God of the Hebrew people, so our countenance should be such as to draw non-believers or tepid followers more closely into the fold that Jesus offers. Additionally we see that Ruth quite willingly leaves her home and possessions behind. In doing that, Ruth continues to model for us a behavior pleasing to Jesus.

This is, in fact, exactly what Jesus requires of us, His disciples. Whatever we know our earthly attachments to be, Jesus calls us to be able to leave them behind. He promises us that, in so doing, our lives will be in keeping with the Father's will. And then, and only then, can we inherit the kingdom of heaven. Our love for Jesus is shown in our everyday words and actions, just as Ruth's love for Naomi and Naomi's God is shown through her everyday words and actions.

We all know that it is fairly easy to make a claim of discipleship. Ruth gives us the courage to make the claim and, as is often said, "walk the talk." Ruth is a beautiful example of witnessing.

Ruth's story continues as she and Naomi move to Bethlehem. Ruth then, living in the town of Bethlehem, finds herself in a position to be the recipient of extreme kindness from a man named Boaz. In Ruth's story we learn of the practice of "redemption." Essentially this custom allows a close relative of a deceased man the option to take care of, or marry, a family member, thus carrying on the family line and "salvaging" or "redeeming" the family name. Boaz was a relative of Elimelech and exercised that option to marry Ruth, Elimelech's daughter-in-law.

With this act comes the true story of our redemption through Christ. Like Ruth, we were "outsiders" to the covenant. And yet we have also been redeemed, just as Ruth was, through Christ's great love for each and every one of us.

With Ruth's marriage to Boaz, another critical piece to our faith-life is put in place. Ruth becomes pregnant and gives birth to Obed. Obed was the father of Jesse, who was the father of David. David, we know is the line from which our Savior will be born. With Ruth's redemption we again witness God's love and His hand in all the lives of those that love and follow Him.

Ruth's story is both simple and yet quite complex. Through her innocent act of love towards her mother-in-law she becomes integral to the family line that will ultimately bring salvation. She teaches us the beauty of a love so pure that it can not escape the imprint of God: a love that we would do well to imitate and bring forth into the world.

Lord,

You loved me enough to send
Your Son,
my Redeemer.

I thank you
and voluntarily accept this redemption.

May I never forget this love.

May I bring that same love into the world.

Like Ruth,
may my words, actions, thoughts, and deeds,
freely given,

be pleasing to You.

Amen

The Word of God

Anyone who loves his father or mother more than me is not worthy of me; anyone who loves his son or daughter more than me is not worthy of me; and anyone who does not take his cross and follow me is not worthy of me. Whoever finds his life will lose it, and whoever loses his life for my sake will find it. Matthew 10:37-39

Then the women said to Naomi, "Blessed is the Lord who has not failed to provide you today with an Heir! May he become famous in Israel! Ruth 4:14

And may the Lord make you increase and abound in love for one another and for all, just as we have for you, 1 Thessalonians 3:1

But Ruth replied, "Don't urge me to leave you or to turn back from you. Where you go I will go, and where you stay I will stay. Your people will be my people and your God my God. Where you die I will die, and there I will be buried. May the Lord deal with me, be it ever so severely, if anything but death separates you and me. When Naomi realized that Ruth was determined to go with her, she stopped urging her. Ruth 1:16-18

But he entered the Most Holy Place once for all by his own blood, having obtained eternal redemption. Hebrews 9:12b

Redemption

You are redeemed through Jesus Christ, your savior. Ruth was redeemed by her deep and abiding love for Naomi. Throughout the week, find ways to show your own abiding love for the people in your own family and, in doing this, remember that you are showing your own abiding love in Jesus who dwells in all. Record some of your feelings this week, as you live in tenderness, so that they will remind you of the depth of the affection Jesus has for you.

_____
_____
_____
_____
_____
_____
_____
_____
_____
_____
_____
_____
_____
_____
_____
_____
_____
_____
_____

A human being, whether male or female, is a person, and therefore, "the only creature on earth which God willed for its own sake;" and at the same time this unique and unrepeatable creature "cannot fully find himself except through the sincere gift of self."

Mulieris Dignitatem

Esther

Dispatches were sent by couriers to all the king's provinces with the order to destroy, kill and annihilate all the Jews-young and old, women and little children-on a single day, the thirteenth day of the twelfth month, the month of Adar, and to plunder their goods. Esther 3:13.

And so it was that Queen Esther found herself in a situation where she was able to bring about the salvation of God's people, the Jews. Esther had been made queen after Queen Vashti disobeyed orders and was removed from her throne. During the process to fill Queen Vashti's position, Esther's Jewish identify was never revealed. But it is her Jewish identify that would play a significant role in her future as queen.

Esther is called upon by her caretaker, Mordecai, to use her position and approach the king regarding the plan against the Jews. At first Esther's response is hesitant but she soon becomes receptive and pours herself wholeheartedly into the task at hand. Esther was, like so many of us have been, in the right place at the right time. And although we may not always recognize God's hand in things, it is there nonetheless. Our lesson from Esther is in seeing how she most assuredly knew how to proceed. She shows us how to move productively in the situations in which God puts us, relying on our faith in Him. Through God's providence Esther became queen and had a role to fill, a purpose to serve. We can certainly see how God's hand was in the details that moved Esther into her position to replace Queen Vashti.

It all began when Queen Vashti disobeyed the king's order to appear before the court. Her disobedience was seen as a possible precedent for other people to disobey the king and so she was removed from her position. It was then suggested that the king *give her royal position to someone else who is better than she. Esther 1:19b.* The king was pleased with this advice and a search began for someone to take Vashti's place. Esther was among the many maidens brought to the harem. She quickly became a favorite due, no doubt, to her beauty and her modest countenance. Like Deborah, Zipporah, and Noah's wife, God would be able to use the self-effacing Esther to do His work. Humility, we know, is a valued trait in Scripture.

When Esther found herself in an elevated position she did not take advantage of it nor deceive herself into believing that it was her "right" or her "due." Instead, we read in Esther 2:15, that she moved cautiously and with great humility.

When the turn came for Esther (the girl Mordecai had adopted, the daughter of his uncle Abihail) to go to the king, she asked for nothing other than what Hegai, the king's eunuch who was in charge of the harem, suggested. And Esther won the favor of everyone who saw her.

Ultimately, Esther is made queen and her role continues to reveal itself as Mordecai approaches her with his request that she speak to the king. When we understand that this jeopardizes her very life, we fully grasp that it is no simple task. Indeed, it takes a great deal of courage for Esther to go to the king. His law was such that anyone approaching him, without first being summoned, risked death. It is easy to see why Esther's first response was one of apprehension. It was when Mordecai pointed out to Esther that her purpose for coming to the role of queen might very well be found in halting the expected tragedy that she accepted the responsibility. Esther 4:16 gives us her response.

"Go, gather together all the Jews who are in Susa, and fast for me. Do not eat or drink for three days, night or day. I and my maids will fast as you do. When this is done, I will go to the king, even though it is against the law. And if I perish, I perish.

Esther reiterates for us the value of intercessory prayer, fasting, and a confidant self-approach to God. She leaves no stone unturned.

Esther had faith in the power of God, just as the woman with a hemorrhage had faith in the power of Jesus. And as did the Canaanite woman whose daughter was possessed. Both these women turned to Christ for their answer. Scripture is filled with women whose strong faith allowed healing to take place, nations to be saved, and wars to be won. Faith, Jesus reminds us, can move mountains.

As the story of Esther continues to unfold we see that she has taken on the task of warding off impending doom against the Hebrews. Through her fasting and praying, and that of her community, she willingly approached the king and was instrumental in stopping the slaughter of the Jews. We also learn that the treacherous Haman, who was the instigator of the plot against the Jews, himself, becomes the victim of his own dishonesty. God has worked all for His good and the good of His people.

Another holy woman who was able to ward off impending doom against God's people was Judith. She is certainly a favorite among many women today as having the admirable traits of beauty (remember this also indicates virtuousness), physical strength, wisdom, and faith. The entire book of Judith (which immediately precedes the story of Esther in the Bible) is a narrative of one woman's ability to follow God, honor Him, and live completely for Him. Judith's story is replete with the message that God can work all things for His good and the good of His people as the first seven chapters of Judith make it known that in every way, God's people were facing the worst of circumstances, the ultimate of enemies. A combination of any and every terrible thing that had come upon them was magnified in the force of Holofernes' command of the situation in which God's people were literally dying of thirst and nearing annihilation.

In Judith's story we are reminded that an ego can be someone's undoing as Holofernes' own ego allows him to listen to Judith's praise of "her Lord" and easily see himself as the object of her worship. Her verbal commitment and continued affirmation of wanting to please her Lord increases Holofernes' vulnerability and ultimately is his demise. Judith, like Esther, is put in a powerful position but does not attribute the position to her own worthiness but to God's mercy and kindness and as such she is His willing instrument reminding us that we can all make that same choice; to be His willing instrument.

Both Judith and Esther are loved today in their roles as women of God and Esther's triumph is still celebrated in the feast of Purim. It reminds the Jews of the remarkable woman who was brave enough to face her own death to save God's people. She is our sister in faith as she reminds us of our own needed bravery to live our Christian faith in the face of rampant secularism. And, like Judith, Esther's complete faith in God carried her through events that seemed impossible.

She teaches us to rely on the intercession of others, the value of fasting and faith, and the need to recognize God's hand in our everyday lives. Esther's story is one of triumph and glory, just as Jesus' resurrection is one of triumph and glory over death. Her story gives us reason to be filled with faith and find strength in that faith. Her story reminds us that we are all handmaids unto the Lord and that He will work in our lives as we allow Him.

Father,

May Esther's faith in You,
and Your hand in her life,
always remind me
of Your interest in my life.

Let my bravery imitate Esther's
as I live a life bolstered by my faith in You
and Your Word.

Please find me in whatever circumstances
are pleasing to You.

Please use me in whatever way
is pleasing to You.

Please guide me so that when
my life on earth is finished
it will have been lived for Your glory.

All these things I ask of You
through Your Son,
My beloved savior,
Jesus Christ.

Amen

The Word of God

When the king's order and edict had been proclaimed, many girls were brought to the citadel of Susa and put under the care of Hegai. Esther also was taken to the king's palace and entrusted to Hegai, who had charge of the harem. Esther 2:8

No one had a bad word to say about her, for she was a very God-fearing woman. Judith 8:8

Instead, whoever wants to become great among you must be your servant, and whoever wants to be first must be slave of all. Mark 10:43b-44

Humility and the fear of the Lord bring wealth and honor and life. Proverbs 22:4

God is not unjust; he will not forget your work and the love you have shown him as you have helped his people and continue to help them. Hebrews 6:10

Judith threw herself down prostrate, with ashes strewn upon her head, and wearing nothing over the sackcloth. While the incense was being offered in the temple of God in Jerusalem that evening, Judith prayed to the Lord with a loud voice. Judith 9:1

God did this so that men would seek him and perhaps reach out for him and find him, though he is not far from each one of us. For in him we live and move and have our being. Acts 17:27-28

Do not reprove me in your anger, Lord, nor punish me in your wrath. Have pity on me, Lord, for I am weak; heal me, Lord, for my bones are trembling. Psalm 6: 2-3

Judith answered him: "Listen to the words of your servant, and let your handmaid speak in your presence! I will tell no lie to my lord this night..." Judith 11:5

Be a Witness

Look for and embrace opportunities this week to spread your faith. In particular seek someone outside of your circle of friends, family, and fellow Christians.

Ask God to bring into your life someone to whom you can be a beacon of light, reflecting Jesus in the most loving of ways.

Consider giving a Christian book, movie, music CD, calendar, plaque, or website to that particular someone this week. In this way you might gently bring the God into his or her life. Consider starting a small prayer group that meets once or twice a month to study the Word and extend an invitation to someone outside your familiar circle of friends and family.

Remember: Share with God your interest in bringing Jesus' love into the world and He will reveal to you an avenue to follow.

We see that through Mary - through her maternal "fiat" ("Let it be done to me") - God begins a New Covenant with humanity. This is the eternal and definitive Covenant in Christ, in his body and blood, in his Cross and Resurrection. Precisely because this Covenant is to be fulfilled "in flesh and blood" its beginning is in the Mother.

Mulieris Dignitatem

Mary

> "Blessed are you who believed that what was spoken to you by the Lord would be fulfilled." Luke 1:45.

With those words, Elizabeth confirms what we already know about Mary, the mother of Jesus: that she freely, and without reservation, trusted in God. With those beautiful words we only begin to fathom the depths of Mary's faith in God. For we know that Mary had all the reason to question and doubt the news as revealed in Luke 1:35.

"The Holy Spirit will come upon you, and the power of the Most High will overshadow you. So the Holy One to be born will be called the Son of God."

As the mother of Jesus, we know that Mary had a tremendous responsibility placed upon her. Her future, our future, was forever changed when she responded to the angel Gabriel, telling him that she considered herself a servant of the Lord. With the acceptance of this life-altering news Mary sets in motion a chain of events that would ultimately provide the only way in which to rectify Eve's transgression. Just as a woman freely rejected God and His will, a woman was needed to freely accept Him and His will. And in so doing, Mary agreed to bring into the world God's answer to our sins.

Upon accepting this role, and having learned of Elizabeth's pregnancy, Mary visits her cousin. It is during this stay that we are privy to Mary and Elizabeth's brief but telling conversation. In those few lines of Scripture we see the absolute love that they share for God and for His purpose in their lives. In Mary's song, often called Mary's Canticle, she gives great praise and honor to God. She recalls His hand in the lives of His people. We are again reminded of God's love towards a humble servant, any modest servant, as Mary says,

"My soul glorifies the Lord and my spirit rejoices in God my Savior, for he has been mindful of the humble state of his servant." Luke 1:46a-48b.

Mary models for us true discipleship of Christ as well as complete obedience to the Father. With this knowledge of her character, God chose Mary to be Jesus' mother. He chose Elizabeth to bear John the Baptist and Mary to bear the Christ Child. In that way, Mary was to serve God and the greater good of God's people. Mary's life clarifies what it means to be a servant of God, what it takes to be a servant of God. She exemplifies for us how we are able to serve God through serving the greater good of all people.

Because of her gentle and unassuming demeanor, God is able to ask anything of Mary. He can count on her cooperation. And as we know He was not asking for a small sacrifice. He was ultimately asking her to sacrifice her son for all humankind. It was a great act of love. It would certainly seem that her love for God, and even her love for us, was bigger than her heartache. This must have been the case for her to have survived such a tragedy. In this way Mary helps us see that it is possible to get outside of ourselves and serve one another in a most glorious way. However, this is both a difficult and often unrewarding earthly task.

Nonetheless, Mary calls us to do just that. She helps us see that in serving God we are helping raise humanity to a level pleasing to Him. Indeed a level planned by Him. We proclaim this in the "Our Father" when we say, *thy will be done, on earth as it is in heaven.* When we mirror Mary's unselfishness, we are able to participate in God's plan for humankind in the most glorious of ways.

As well as being the one chosen to carry the Christ child, we should remember that Mary was Jewish. She most definitely would have enriched Jesus' life with the Jewish celebrations of Yom Kippur, Chanukah, the Sabbath, and Passover. From this perspective, the birth of Jesus provided a means for God to offer salvation to His own people. It then tied Gentiles to Jews in a deep and abiding way, as Gentiles soon began to acknowledge the Jewish Messiah as the Son of God.

Our Christian faith, then, evolved from the Jewish faith and has its origins in the faith that worshipped the one true God. For us, as Christians, He is the God who sent the Son.

While Christians recognize a need to claim Jesus as Lord and Savior, we also should recognize the gift we have received from the Jewish people. Jews, like Christians, have seen persecution and intolerance for thousands of years. The Jewish people held on to the belief in the one true God while pagan nations attempted to destroy and conquer the Jewish race. Through women like Esther, Deborah, Noah's wife, and Mary, the Jewish faith survived in such as way as to bring the Messiah.

Finally, we recognize Mary as one of the first disciples. As obedient as she was to God, she was also a faithful follower of Christ. She set an example for us, showing us how to live and abide in His ways. Mary shows us what true discipleship necessitates. From her life we know that, as disciples of Christ, there will be pain and sorrow along with joy and gladness. The depth of one allows us the full exultation of the other just as the horror of the crucifixion allowed for the glory of the resurrection. They go hand in hand.

Discipleship includes times of upheaval and periods of grace. At the heart of discipleship is the transforming love of Jesus: a love that can forever change us. It is this all-encompassing love that allows us to share in each other's lives in the richest of ways. Without love, as St. Paul tells us, we are just clanging symbols. Jesus showed us, through His tender words and charitable deeds, how to love one another in a manner that pleases God. And, of course, Mary's love for the Father allowed us to know the Son, our only way to the Father. Through it all, Mary gives us a beautiful example of a discipleship that is based on such love.

Undoubtedly, there are certainly many, many things we can do in life without love. But without love, they would all be meaningless, empty acts. We might even get very far with our egos leading the way. But nothing will change the fact that God's love, as given to us in His Son, is our only means of salvation. It all begins and ends with this devotion. It is placed before us to freely choose or reject. It is a love that Mary most certainly had.

Indeed, it was Christ's love for us that allowed Him to suffer and endure death on a cross. It was God's love for us that allowed Him to consider offering up His Son for us. And it is our love for one another that allows us to be all that God intends us to be.

Like so many women whose stories are told in Scripture, Mary gives us courage to embrace God's will with enthusiasm and confidence. She shows us that being a loving servant to God means being a beacon of light to all women. She had a unique role to fill and did so with a heart full of devotion. In saying "yes" to Gabriel she said "yes" to each and every one of us.

While Mary's gift of free will was no more, or no less, than Eve's or yours or mine; the way she used it was different, indeed. Finding herself in the most difficult of circumstances to understand, she relied solely and completely on God. In that way she becomes an example for us to do the same. Then, as the mother of Christ, she continued to be an example of selfless love, always directing us to her Son as she did the servants at the Wedding of Cana when she said, "Do as he tells you." We honor her in her role and are grateful for her continued direction to her Son, who gives us life.

The world gives us many ways to practice greed, envy, and trickery. We live in a society that values notoriety and fame. We are encouraged to value what is **in** this world while Scripture tells us we aren't even **of** this world. Mary, then, in the most gentle of ways, reminds us the value of selfless love. Her benevolence helps us recognize that our very existence is, and was always intended to be, an expression of love.

Lord of All,

Mary reminds me what it truly means to serve a purpose
apart from my own interest.

Help me this day to heed Your call.

Consider me a handmaid unto You.

Give me the courage of Mary to serve You
in ways I can't even imagine.

Allow me to know that my life is pleasing to You.

I ask this all through
Your Blessed Son,
My Savior, Jesus,
Your Anointed One.

Amen

The Word of God

Grace, mercy and peace from God the Father and from Jesus Christ, the Father's Son, will be with us in truth and love. 2 John 3

And the God of love and peace will be with you. 2 Corinthians 13:11

If I speak in the tongues of men and of angels, but have not love, I am only a resounding gong or a clanging symbol. If I have the gift of prophecy and can fathom all mysteries and all knowledge, and if I have faith that can move mountains, but have not love, I am nothing. If I give all I possess to the poor and surrender my body to the flames, but have not love, I gain nothing. 1 Corinthians 13:1-3

Then Simeon blessed them and said to Mary, his mother; "This child is destined to cause the falling and rising of many in Israel, and to be a sign that will be spoken against, so that the thoughts of many hearts will be revealed. And a sword will pierce your own soul too." Luke 2:34-35

But the angel said to her, "Do not be afraid, Mary, you have found favor with God. You will be with child and give birth to a son, and you are to give him the name Jesus. He will be great and will be called the Son of the Most High. The Lord God will give him the throne of his *father David, and he will reign over the house of Jacob forever; his kingdom will never end. Luke 1:30-33*

God created man in his image, in the divine image he created him; male and female he created them. Genesis 1:27

David built houses for himself in the City of David and prepared a place for the ark of God, pitching a tent for it there. 1Chronicles 15:1

Come and see the works of the Lord, who has done fearsome deed on earth. Psalm 46:9

Trust in the Lord, your God, and you will be found firm. Trust in his prophets and you will succeed. 2 Chronicles 20:20b

The Greater Good of God's People

This week your focus is to "get outside of yourself." Ideally our hearts are filled with love and kindness and our emotions are that of support, gratitude, and encouragement. However, we often find ourselves concentrating more on our perspective of things than we should. Mary taught us to consider others first, and in so doing, serving God.

During your quiet time with God, ask Him to place upon your heart someone with whom you need repair or strengthen ties. Let the Holy Spirit guide you as you ask the Lord to open your heart to His wishes.

When we take a real interest in serving God we are able to let His love shine through in our words and actions. Combine all the scripture lessons this week so that you may forge ahead to do God's will in the world and bring about His greater good. It all begins with one simple act of kindness. God bless you and anoint your journey.

Christ is the bridegroom of the Church – the Church is the Bride of Christ.

Mulieris Dignitatem

Mary Magdalene

From start to finish, Mary Magdalene seems to be the quintessential female for today's Christian woman. We know that Jesus came here for sinners: she was a sinner. We know that Jesus came here looking to forgive sins: she accepted His forgiveness. And we know that Jesus came here looking for believers: she believed unequivocally. Scripture also lets us know that Mary Magdalene helped support Jesus' ministry and was so faithful that she followed Him to His crucifixion. Finally, she was the one to whom He chose to show Himself upon His resurrection. And so, it seems as if we have a lot to learn from her.

Early on we learn from Eve's story the reality of sin and the need for repentance. Mary Magdalene seems to embody that message. She accepted Jesus' forgiveness and freely chose to follow Him. Like many women are unable to do, it seems as if Mary Magdalene found a great ability to move forward in Jesus' healing and forgiveness. She did not look back but instead kept her focus on Jesus' teachings and the courage that gave her to forge ahead. According to Scripture, she was also interested in helping others know and accept Him. We find, in Luke 8:1b-3, that Mary Magdalene, Joanna, and Susanna had been cured by Jesus and were, in fact, supporting Him in His ministry.

> *The twelve were with him, and also some women who had been cured of evil spirits and diseases: Mary (called Magdalene) from whom seven demons had come out; Joanna the wife of Cuza, the manager of Herod's household; Susanna; and many others. These women were helping to support them out of their own means.*

Along with supporting Him during His mission on earth, Mary Magdalene was also at His death. She stood at a distance during the crucifixion and was there as the earth trembled and rocks broke apart. She must have heard the centurion exclaim what she already knew in her heart, *"Surely he was the Son of God!" Matthew 27:54b.* We have to admire her bravery as well as her faithfulness. We know that many followers feared for their lives and thus avoided the scene at Calgary. Her story reveals to us the power of complete faith. It allows us, in the face of whatever difficulty we might have to confront, to be able to replace fear with hope and courage. And as we know, His death did not stop her devotion. It was Mary Magdalene who prepared spices to anoint His crucified body.

Not only was she a devoted follower of Jesus' but her trust was so deep, so strong that she is to whom the Lord appeared upon His resurrection! She was the first to acknowledge, accept, and witness to our Risen Lord.

When we consider that our faith rests upon the Lord's resurrection, and it was to Mary Magdalene that He chose to first appear, we know that she must be a role model of the faithfulness for us. Throughout the Old and New Testament faith, like wisdom, is a valued and sought after trait. Indeed, when we go back and consider how God knew that Noah's wife would be up to the arduous task on the ark, or that Zipporah would trustfully support Moses, we have to assume that He also knew Mary Magdalene had the faith to witness His Son's resurrection.

When we hear the recounting of Mary Magdalene, Joanna, and Mary (the mother of James) sharing their knowledge of the risen Lord it seems evident why women were chosen for this momentous occasion. As these women tell the eleven apostles their experience at the empty tomb we hear that they were not believed. Only Peter ran to see if there was any truth to their tale. The other men considered the story "nonsense." As much as these men loved and followed Jesus, we have to wonder what their responses might have been at the empty tomb. In this interesting exchange we come to see how men and women must work together for the Lord, each bringing his or her own piece to the intricate puzzle of life.

Certainly it has been our experience that women, as mentioned in the earlier section, "Holy Spirit," have a particular intuition in which the Lord works with them. This doesn't presume that men are without gifts in which they, too, work with God. More pointedly, it restates that women have a connection to God in a different manner then men. And we should never underestimate how much God depends on both relationships: male and female. This simply reiterates the fact that when we get caught up in a secular message that calls us to aspire to, as equals, all that men pursue, we might lose sight of what God wants us to seek. And we will also lose sight of how God wants us to do our seeking.

In retrospect we clearly see that a faithful woman was able to receive the Risen Lord and witness to disbelieving men. But then, upon accepting this fact, these same men were able to go into the world and spread the Good News in ways that were probably unavailable to women. This understanding allows us to welcome God's plan with knowledge that each and every one of us will play a necessary and vital part in the building of His kingdom.

Together, men and women are able to bring to this world the message of eternal life with Christ. This reality teaches us all to be hopeful, jubilant and tenacious. Indeed, our belief in the salvation of Christ, and its accompanying joy, is the biggest banner we can wave. The way we live, the attitudes we take into the world and the light we reveal is the most significant testament we can give as we persevere in life. These aren't things we keep sequestered in our hearts but are, instead, realities that we bring into the world. What Jesus tells us in Matthew 25:40 should guide our everyday lives.

The King will reply, "I tell you the truth, whatever you did for one of the least of these brothers of mine, you did for me."

So in Mary Magdalene we have a very real example for today's Christian woman. She gives us conviction to accept Jesus' forgiveness and to courageously follow Him. We are encouraged to be all that we can be through His gift of salvation. As the first witness to His resurrection, she inspires us to be the faithful witnesses that He calls each of us to be, both in our hearts and in our lives.

Lord of all,

May Your Son's resurrection
never cease to enthrall me.

May I be inspired,
with each new day,
to be resurrected in Your love.

When I am weary
or lonesome,

Let my faith and courage
come from knowing
that You are ever at my side.

When I am joyful and at peace,

let my gratitude come from knowing
that You are the source
of all good things.

When my time on earth is done,
let Your warm embrace
and loving smile
welcome me home.

All things,
through Christ,
The Way.

Amen

The Word of God

Early on the first day of the week, while it was still dark, Mary Magdalene went to the tomb and saw that the stone had been removed from the entrance. John 20:1

At this, she turned around and saw Jesus standing there, but she did not realize that it was Jesus. "Woman," he said, "why are you crying? Who is it you are looking for?" Thinking he was the gardener, she said, "Sir, if you have carried him away, tell me where you have put him, and I will get him." Jesus said to her, "Mary." She turned toward him and cried out in Aramaic, "Rabboni!" (which means teacher). John 20:14-16

Mary Magdalene went to the disciples with the news: "I have seen the Lord!" John 20: 18a

Be joyful always; pray continually; give thanks in all circumstances, for this is God's will for you in Christ Jesus. 1 Thessalonians 5:16-18

Jesus turned and saw her, "Take heart, daughter," he said, "your faith has healed you." And the woman was healed from that moment. Matthew 9:22

Then Jesus answered, "Woman, you have great faith! Your request is granted." And her daughter was healed from that very hour. Matthew 15:28

The Sabbath

Mary Magdalene is our call to embrace the Sabbath as God intended. She was the first to see the risen Lord and, as such, gives us a responsibility to usher in and observe the Sabbath in richer ways. As Christians we consider Sunday to be a weekly celebration of His resurrection as well as a day the Lord set aside.

This Sunday, and all Sundays that follow, look for ways to institute, or re-institute, the sanctity of the Sabbath in your home and with your family and friends. If you were blessed with parents or grandparents who had a home altar, a kneeler, or simply lit candles by a window overlooking the garden, consider ways to bring these anointed reminders into you own home and encourage each member of your family to spend a few "quiet, Sabbath minutes with God" in addition to time spent at Mass.

If Sunday has always been your day to catch up on laundry, do grocery shopping, or attend a mix of soccer matches and basketball games, consider slowly changing your schedule so that the Sabbath will become the day the Lord set aside for you and Him. Let Him know that you want to make Him a priority and He will help that happen!

If Sunday has always been your day to spend with Lord, renew that commitment by asking Him if you have an area in your life that He would like you to meditate upon. Spend extra time in His word. Spend additional time in His home. These will open those lines of communication in untold ways.

Enjoy each Sabbath as God intended: joyfully and with great faith in the Risen Lord.

For Christ has redeemed all without exception.

Mulieris Dignitatem

Scripture's Messages

From Eve to Mary we look at women of Scripture and extract their messages to us. They teach us that God's blessings are boundless and that when we use our free will to both accept the salvation of Jesus and offer up our repentant hearts, we live lives most pleasing to God. We see that we will experience a variety of seasons, all working for the good of His plan. There are times when we will be strong and times when we will be weak. Through them all we are able to serve God and our reason for living.

We understand from Eve the consequences of sin and from Noah's wife the need to serve God and others in a joyful and diligent way. Sarah teaches us to turn impatience and jealousy into gratitude and faith in God's promises. She shows us the very human characteristics of envy and anxiousness and allows us to bask in God's commitment to us when we are less than what He would like us to be. Thus, encouraging us all the more to be godly women.

Leah's life and place as a powerful matriarch of the faith calls us to look at how our lives were meant to glorify His kingdom. In tuned to the Spirit, Leah teaches us to develop those same gifts of the Spirit that allow us to answer His call.

Lot's wife reminds us that it is harmful to give our future to the past and rob God of our "todays." Rebekah's story instills in us the need for intercessory prayer while Rachel's strength gives us encouragement to call upon God with our own needs and desires. Shiphrah and Puah remind us of God's natural law placed upon our hearts and the rewards for responding to it.

Zipporah challenges us to respond to God's call even when it is in stark contrast to what we have imagined for ourselves and to cherish the ways we might support our loved ones in their own journeys. Deborah shows us how to yield power in a way that is pleasing to God and yet productive in our earthly existence. Ruth, a Moabite woman, foreshadows our own purchase by the blood of Jesus Christ.

From Miriam we continue to see that even in the midst of God's graces we are able to fall prey to earthly temptations of envy and ungratefulness. But, also as importantly, we see from Miriam how powerfully we can serve God when we inspire and encourage one another.

Esther helps us wield whatever power God has given us for His good and the good of His people, our brethren. Mary, the mother of Jesus, was the embodiment of the love that God looked for in humankind. She is the role model of discipleship and a link to our sisters in faith. Mary Magdalene renews our understanding of why Jesus became man: to forgive our sins and to give us eternal life.

All women in Scripture, from those named to those unnamed, show us how we are uniquely called to honor God, Jesus, and the Holy Spirit all our days.

Father,

Let my mind be renewed by Your Word
and my heart renewed by Your Spirit.

Let my life be a reflection of
Your light into the world.

May all my words be wise ones
and my actions compassionate.

When You call upon me may my ear be inclined
and my response swift.

I belong solely to You And live for Your glory

Through Christ, now and forever

Amen

The Word of God

For the grace of God that brings salvation has appeared to all men. It teaches us to say "No" to ungodliness and worldly passions, and to live self-controlled, upright and godly lives in this present age, while we wait for the blessed hope-the glorious appearing of our great God and Savior, Jesus Christ, who gave himself for us to redeem us from all wickedness and to purify for himself a people that are his very own, eager to do what is good. Titus 2:11-14

The seed is the word of God. Those along the path are the ones who hear, and then the devil comes and takes away the word from their hearts, so that they may not believe and be saved. Those on the rock are the ones who receive the word with joy when they hear it, but they have no root. They believe for a while, but in the time of testing they fall away. The seed that fell among thorns stands for those who hear, but as they go on their way they are choked by life's worries, riches, and pleasures, and they do not mature. But the seed on good soil stands for those with a noble and good heart, who hear the word, retain it, and by persevering produce a good crop. Luke 8:11-15

Many women were there, watching from a distance. They had followed Jesus from Galilee to care for his needs. Matthew 27:55

Let those who love the Lord hate evil, for he guards the lives of his faithful ones and delivers them from the hand of the wicked. Psalm 97:10

If you wish to return, O Israel, say the Lord, return to me. Jeremiah 4:1

Hear, O Lord, for you are a God of mercy; and have mercy on us, who have sinned against you; for you are enthroned forever, while we are perishing forever. Baruch 3:3

Your Time on Earth

God gave us this fleeting time on earth to accomplish a mission. That mission is to spread His love and His Word to the ends of the earth. He gives us a variety of ways to accomplish this mission and innumerable lessons to learn along the way.

The intent of this book, and its related activities, is to inspire you to do just that: to be a living witness to God's goodness and the salvation of Christ: even to examine your life through Christ's eyes. It is to inspire you to meditate upon the Word of God each and every day. To study it, embrace it, and make it alive in your life.

One day we will each stand before God and give an accounting of our days. Let us be well prepared for that conversation so that we may enjoy His presence for eternity.

Challenge yourself every day to bring love and light into the world. Every day is, truly, a gift from God in which you can accomplish great things in even the smallest of tasks.

Look at each day as a new opportunity to ask yourself questions that will help you grow as a Christian. Consider the list just a starting point.

You might create a list to begin your day and restate the questions for an end-of-day examination.

Look at the list started here and then create your own list or lists.

- ✓ What is He encouraging me to do?
- ✓ Who is in my life and for what reason?
- ✓ How can I serve Him today?
- ✓ Do I have a grateful attitude?
- ✓ Do I encourage and welcome the guidance of the Holy Spirit?
- ✓ Am I persevering with faith in Him?
- ✓ Am I joyfully pursuing my purpose?

Faith, trust, and learning God's Word will help you answer these questions, enjoy your journey, and bear great fruit.

May all the days of your life be filled with the grace and peace of Christ. May they allow you opportunities to grow as a Christian and to fulfill God's purpose for you. May you find the Lord's favor within your family, at home, work, and in your community. And may you always remember that there are no coincidences in God's plan when the Holy Spirit is guiding you.

God bless you in all you do as you bring His love and light into the world.

Printed in the United States
121267LV00003B/334/P